Merry
Old Mobiles
On Parade

by *Hi Sibley*

DISTRIBUTED BY

GARDEN CITY BOOKS, GARDEN CITY, NEW YORK

INTRODUCTION

Your sweet - running automobile of today affords a lot of pleasure, but is it ever exciting? Its pioneer ancestors most certainly were. Fifty years ago, if your noisy little machine could climb a certain hill near your home you were the envy of the owners of less able vehicles, and could you make a round trip to a neighboring town twenty-five or thirty miles distant, without engine or tire trouble, all in the same day, you were a man of distinction. And how you bragged about it!

My own introduction to the Roaring Road as a youngster in 1901 was aboard a tiny, toboggan-dash Oldsmobile. It had a single cylinder of four-and-a-half horsepower that cranked from the seat; it could do twenty miles an hour on the level, twenty-five on a slight down grade with a following wind, but with the buggy-top raised a strong adverse gust could stall it completely.

An indulgent father let me spend all my waking hours out of school chugging up one paved street of South Bend and down another, over and over, until one housewife told my mother that she could set her clock by me, as I passed her house regularly every thirty minutes, on the hour.

With the steering tiller I had to lean far out to one side or another to make sharp turns, and this arrangement proved awkward on one occasion. Father had delegated me to pick up a business acquaintance at the railroad station, a huge man who was almost as wide as he was tall. As he climbed into the little Olds, it sagged perilously on that side, and his paunch bulged out so far I couldn't get the tiller past it to make a right-hand turn, and had to maneuver all the way back to the office with left-hand turns only. Fortunately there were no one-way streets and I could park on either side.

That Olds was really a good car, sturdy and willing, and we were not fair-weather tourists —we penetrated to the FAR places. I vividly recall a journey of forty miles from South Bend to Benton Harbor, Michigan, in 1902. There were four of us in, or rather on that over - taxed machine; father and mother in front and sister and myself on the dos-a-dos seat in back, together with a big lunch basket, hammock, garden tools and other equipment for opening up our cottage. It took us from seven in the morning to supper time, with stopping for frenzied horses, pushing up hills and through sand, fixing a puncture and tightening the clutch, but when we arrived intact at the lake we were   dis- covering the Pacific.   eve it was he first car seen in Benton Harbor.

Other early models f llowed the Oldsmobile in our family, a 1904 Franklin, Ford Model "N," forerunner of the Model "T," 1902 Perfection (that name was somewhat on the extravagant side), a trim little 1908 Hupp runabout, 1909 Reo, 1910 Hudson, Waverly Electric, Detroit Electric, and progressively several well-known makes up to the present.

Discussion of pioneer motor vehicles will always be controversial. This book is not concerned with who built the first successful automobile in this country, which was the first equipped with a steering wheel, the exact date that shaft drive superseded chain, or any of the other firsts; rather it is merely to display some of the forerunners of our sleek modern cars and a few of their individual features. Up to 1905 scarcely any two makes were alike, which fact made them especially interesting. On some early models where records are not available I have had to rely on my memory, a lively one if not infallible. And if you find the anecdotes rich in corn, bear in mind that they were born over forty years ago and at that period, in our simple-minded way, we thought them amusing.

Hi Sibley

Carriages without horses shall go,
And accidents fill the world with woe.

Old Mother Shipton has been vindicated insofar as this part of her prophecy is concerned. Of course, it is now generally believed that the verse, of which the foregoing is only a part, was a hoax to the extent that the predictions were circulated after most of the things had come to pass.

But it must be admitted that the author of the introductory lines anticipated present-day traffic problems. The comic sketch here shown appeared in 1828 shortly after the advent of steam carriages which was nearly four centuries after Mother Shipton is supposed to have lived. The artist was himself something of a seer because he attempted to show how the streets would some day be clogged by horseless carriages.

CUGNOT 1769

In that year Capt. Nicolas Joseph Cugnot built a ponderous military tractor, on the single front wheel of which was mounted the boiler and engine, and to steer it the entire load had to be turned by means of a handlebar similar to that of a bicycle. Two single-acting cylinders drove the front wheel through a ratchet at a speed of about two miles an hour, and the steam supply lasted a little over ten minutes. Incredible as it may seem, at that snail's pace it ran into a stone wall and was wrecked. A second vehicle was constructed in 1770 after this same design and the vehicle is still being preserved today in the Conservatoire National des Arts et Metiers in Paris.

CUGNOT'S VEHICLE OF 1770.   (Courtesy Smithsonian Institution)

50 Centuries of Auto Development

Prior to 1900 the automobile was as much of a novelty to the American public as space ships are today, and very few persons had seen one in spite of the fact that the history of self-propelled vehicles in this country alone began one hundred and forty-five years ago. The original world pioneer was Cugnot of France who built his cumbersome steam tractor in 1769. Ten steam coaches, forerunners of the motor bus, operated profitably in England from 1828 to 1838.

So, by no means did the automobile pop up all at once—or even in one man's lifetime; it was a slow and gradual development, literally through the Ages. To record the various contributors to this modern chariot we must start with the hairy biped of prehistoric times who first hacked off a round slice of log and used it as a wheel, and the cave man who melted

ore and cast spear heads in clay molds; we must include our own Ben Franklin with his key-and-kite-string discovery of the jump spark (remember how we youngsters rediscovered it by shuffling across the Brussels carpet on frosty evenings and touching a finger to the tip of sleeping kitty's ear, with sprightly results?) Most important, too, is Goodyear who accidentally learned how to vulcanize rubber when he slopped over some sulphur onto a gob of gutta percha on a hot stove (and what an untidy fellow he must have been around the kitchen). Then there was cotton-gin inventor Eli Whitney who introduced mass production; the invention of the four-cycle internal combustion engine by Otto, a German, etc., etc.

And—most amazing—a patent was granted to a lone man on an internal combustion vehicle; the Selden patent shown on page 7.

OLIVER EVANS' "ORUKTER AMPHIBOLOS"——1805.

An American engineer, Oliver Evans, built a steam dredge in 1805 for operation in the harbor at Philadelphia, and to get it to the water from the place of construction mounted the scow on wheels and hooked up the power. It weighed twenty-tons and was not exactly

speedy, but nevertheless takes its place as the first American-built self-propelled vehicle, and actually our first amphibian. The wheels were removed for launching. Photograph is of model constructed by Mr. Greville Bathe of Philadelphia and St. Augustine.

OLIVER EVANS' "ORUKTER AMPHIBOLOS." ORIGINAL MACHINE BUILT IN 1805.

GURNEY 1829

An Englishman, Sir Goldsworthy Gurney, produced a number of steam coaches, one of which is said to have made the round trip between London and Bath in 1829, covering the 200 miles at the rate of 15 miles an hour. This report should be taken with a large dose of salt, for even over hard-surfaced Roman roads it is doubtful that the ponderous vehicles of that era could have done better than eight or ten miles an hour. It must be remembered that the Duryea gas car in the Times-Herald race in Chicago in 1895 averaged only 7 1/2 miles an hour, running time.

(Courtesy Smithsonian Institution)

GURNEY STEAM COACH—1829

CHURCH'S STEAM COACH 1832

If the builders put as much time on the mechanism as they did on the paint job, this steam coach must have been a bit of all right. A fleet of these elegant carriers operated between London and Birmingham in 1832, but they were abandoned on account of competition from the railroads. Other lines were forced out of business because of heavy tolls on this type of road vehicle and in 1865 they received the K.O. when an act was passed that restricted them to four miles an hour in the country, two in the city, and a man with a red flag had to precede the vehicle. There were no Hot Rods on the highways. Not until 1903 was the speed limit raised to 20 m.p.h.; the red flag had been chucked a few years earlier.

(Smithsonian Institution Photo)

STEAM VEHICLE OF WILLIAM CHURCH—1832

AUSTIN 1863

One of the first, if not THE first, steam vehicles built for private use was this English Austin of 1863. The long pistons drove direct on the crankshaft-rear-axle, after the manner of a locomotive. The water tank was in back, boiler under seat with glass tube water gauge at the side. Note the frail steering handle, and the throttle protruding from the floorboard.

(Edison Institute Photo)

5

WOODCUT OF RICHARD DUDGEON'S STEAM VEHICLE OF ABOUT 1868. THE ORIGINAL VEHICLE IS TODAY OWNED BY MR. GEORGE WATERMAN, JR., PROVIDENCE, R. I.

RICHARD DUDGEON 1868.

Four years after the Civil War Richard Dudgeon of New York built a steam "carry-all" with a capacity of ten passengers. It had solid wooden wheels and with its horizontal boiler, smoke stack and cylinders on the side resembled a railroad locomotive. This ma-chine, which is shown in the drawing at the top of this page, is on exhibition at the Belcourt Museum, Newport, Rhode Island, and is still in good operating condition. It is believed to be the earliest surviving self-propelled vehicle in this country.

HERE IS A REAL pioneer among gasoline cars, this one-cylinder vehicle built by Siegfried Marcus in Vienna in 1875, and preserved in the Technisches Museum in that city.

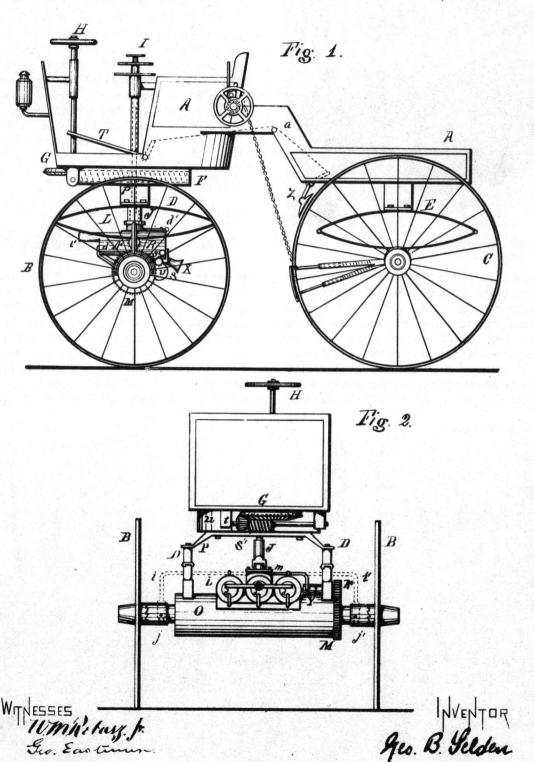

Fig. 1.

Fig. 2.

WITNESSES

INVENTOR

Geo. B. Selden

PATENT ON INTERNAL COMBUSTION ENGINE GRANTED TO G. B. SELDEN IN 1895.

G. B. SELDEN 1879

Here is a patent office model of 1879 submitted by George B. Selden of Rochester, New York, whose application was kept "in solution" by one means or another until a patent was granted in 1895. The patents were acquired by a syndicate organized for the purpose and called the Association of Licensed Automobile Manufacturers, which demanded —and received—royalties from many manufacturers, and threatened suit against those who did not kick in. One non-kicker-in was Henry Ford, and after years of litigation he won his case and the A. L. A. M. was dissolved. Around 1905 a full-sized version of this vehicle was built as an exhibit for the court while the famous suit was underway. That full-size vehicle is now at the Stevens Institute of Technology, Hoboken, New Jersey, and the model in the collection of the U. S. National Museum, Washington, D. C.

(Smithsonian Institution Photo)

SELDEN PATENT OFFICE MODEL, 1879

BENZ "VELOCIPEDE" 1892

Benz "Velocipede" of 1892 had cone pulleys with belts for speed changes, same as on an old-style engine lathe. There was quite a handful of levers on that vertical steering post to think about in an emergency. Note four-tone bulb horn.

(Edison Institute Photo)

GERMAN BENZ 1892

The fringe-top surrey goes mechanical.
This 1892 German Benz phaeton had practically
the same power plant and chassis as the
"Velocipede" shown in the preceding illustration. A belt-speed-change car was featured
in "The Lightning Conductor" by C. N. and
A. N. Williamson, a novel about motoring
abroad in 1902.

(Edison Institute Photo)

DURYEA 1893

This Duryea horseless carriage, built in
1893, is one of the contestants in the "first
automobile built in America." It had a one-
cylinder, four h.p. engine mounted horizontally
under the carriage body. Drive chain not
shown in this photograph.

(Smithsonian Institution Photos)

HAYNES 1893

This 1893 Haynes is another contender for
the "First car built in America" title. On
its trial trip July 4, 1894, it made 7 m.p.h.
The design was conceived by Elwood Haynes,
a utility executive, who tired of driving over
his territory behind a slow horse, and com-
missioned the Apperson Brothers to build it.
It is distinctly a carriage with power mechanism mounted below, a two h.p. two-cycle Sintz
gas engine.

STEPHEN BALZER 1894

This unique little vehicle on bicycle wheels was driven by a three-cylinder rotary, air-cooled engine. It appears that the whirling power plant might singe the driver's calves when in action. It was built by Stephen M. Balzer in New York in 1894.

(Smithsonian Institution Photo)

Strange New Word—"AUTO – MOBILE"

My first acquaintance with the term "auto-mobile" was through a Youth's Companion story, issue of July 16, 1896. Although obviously fiction, the author had attempted to describe a motor vehicle with fantastic results. I quote:

"What I saw on the open ground in the rear of the stable may be described superficially as a vehicle of four wheels with large pneumatic rubber tires upon which was mounted a long, airy-looking platform. In advance of the forward wheels and connected with them by a kind of 'tongue' was another wheel, some-what like the forward wheel of a bicycle, provided with a steering head and a seat behind for the driver, engineer or steersman.

"Beneath the platform was a small, ovoid tank, cylinder and piston rod, the latter connecting with the rear pair of large wheels by means of a crank axle. In short, it was a little gasoline engine, in which, however, kerosene oil could be used if preferred.

"A tiny stream of oil trickled through a little pipe to the cylinder and there it was burned, teaspoonful by teaspoonful, to make the power. It was ignited by the flame of a little lamp protected by glass, like a lantern. The engineer or steersman from his seat behind the steering wheel (meaning the front wheel; it was steered by bicycle handlebars: author) could shut the oil off or turn it on at will."

Just as simple as that. Note that the "piston rod" acted directly on the rear axle, (as in a steam locomotive) and the engine developed four h. p. One might anticipate a slight knock in getting under way or climbing a grade. But quite the contrary, as we shall see.

Four H. P. Runs Away With A Moving Van

The author further stated that the "Auto-Mobile" as he spelled it, could carry all the load one wanted, provisions for six months

A NARROW SHAVE

and go to San Francisco and back. It had a top speed of 20 miles an hour, but the reader was reassured "the pace was not disquieting to one used to steam car speeds" (i.e. the railroad). The inventor treated the intrepid author to a demonstration which nearly stilled his typewriting fingers forever when the "cut-off rod jammed" and they couldn't stop; ahead was a long hill which "the Auto-Mobile began to ascend at full speed and finally, after close shaves with several hayracks, bridges and gyrating Percherons, they plunged into a thicket of soft pine shrubs and lived to tell the tale.

Now as ridiculous as that seems in the light of present motor development, it got by with the juvenile readers, for that author's sketchy knowledge of such a vehicle was Phi Beta Kappa rating compared to what they knew. In fact, the description left such an indelible impression in my memory that forty years later I was able to give the approximate date it appeared to the publishers and through the courtesy of Mr. Franklin T. Reck, Managing Editor, obtain a photostatic copy from which I have quoted.

I suspect that author had had a brief look at Hiram Maxim's motor-tricycle built for the Pope Manufacturing Company, Hartford, Connecticut, and put on the market that year as a package delivery unit. Maxim's machine was driven by a small air-cooled engine with hot tube ignition mounted on the rear end, but instead of the practically impossible "piston rod acting on a crank axle" was equipped with clutch and gearshift. A long platform or parcel carrier something like that described in the story extended out in front. Maxim controlled his machine from the back.

(Smithsonian Institution Photo)

HARRY A. KNOX, of Springfield, Massachusetts, built this three-wheeler in 1899, and had helped build Duryea cars in 1896 when their output was 13 vehicles. It had a "porcupine cylinder," a large number of small rods being screwed in to radiate heat. Bore was 4 1/2 in. and stroke 8 in., an unusually long one. It was rated 8 h.p.

THIS 1898 WINTON Horseless Carriage was the first automobile sold by the Winton Motor Carriage Co., to Robert Allison of Port Carbon, Pennsylvania, but was NOT the first automobile sold in the United States, as has been so often claimed. It is one of the first of a long line of American motor vehicles that included 1,876 different makes. Out of that vast cavalcade only a score or so have survived.

This car is now in the collection of the U. S. National Museum, Washington, D. C.

NAMES, NAMES, NAMES!

Did you ever hear of a Dile, Mora, Parenti or Serrifile?

These were once-hopeful motor cars, a few of the two-thousand-odd that have passed over the hill since Alexander Winton sold his first horseless carriage fifty-two years ago. Most of them had to be pushed to the top, but they managed the rest of the trip to Oblivion with dispatch.

A carnival of names; who today remembers the Ajax, Black Crow, Centaur, De Tamble, Pungs-Finch or Wheel-Within-Wheel? There was a good poker hand in the Ace, King, Queen and Jaxon, and a sizeable zoo included a Deere, Colt, Dragon, Lion, Wolf and Wolverine. No Horse was listed but one enterprising inventor actually attached a wooden horse head to his dashboard to reassure doubting Dobbins along the highway.

There was even a HENRY not built by Ford.

Some pioneers strove to inspire confidence in their product with such names as the Rapid, the Glide and the Long Distance of 1902—a period when any distance covered was something of an achievement. Modesty was ignored in the Success, Marvel, Great and the Only. On the other hand, one non-too-optimistic genius conceded the inevitable right at the start by naming his creation the Dodo.

(Courtesy Packard Motor Car Co.)

THE FIRST PACKARD, built at Warren, Ohio, in 1899. It is a one-cylinder model with tiller steering. Note sturdy steering knuckles, elaborate front spring arrangement and nifty carving effect on side, below seat. Body NOT by Fisher.

(Courtesy Smithsonian Institution)

OLDS GASOLINE AUTOMOBILE 1897

This is not an Oldsmobile, as that name had not been coined in 1897, nor is it the first Olds gasoline automobile, which was destroyed by fire. Four of these were made, with a single-cylinder six horsepower horizontal engine installed beneath the carriage body, driving it at about ten miles an hour with four passengers. Speed selection was provided by three friction clutches controlled by the crank handle at the right of the driver, giving two forward speeds and one reverse. The radiator consisted of 21 horizontal tubes mounted flat against the underside of the body. This same arrangement was used in the first curved-dash Oldsmobile. Neither one had cooling fins.

PACKARD

Grand Old Man of Packard was Henry B. Joy; you might say he was THE Packard Company for, although the name was taken from James Ward Packard, the founder of Warren, Ohio, it was Mr. Joy's ability and persistence that brought the struggling young concern through its infant years, the first of which put them $200,000 in the red. It was his custom, after the company was well on its feet, to take new models on long tours and "give 'em hell." His route could be followed by the wires he sent back to the engineering department: "Make such-and-such a part heavier or "Unit Number so-and-so is all wrong period redesign" until by the time he got back full of constructive experience, the experimental model might have a score of proposed improvements.

His interest in the Packard began in New York where he had gone with a relative to pick out an automobile for his own use. The first machine he looked at was a steam runabout, but while the mechanic was getting up pressure the water glass burst. Joy and companion left hastily. Out on Broadway fire engines were galloping by, and a man rushed out of a salesroom to crank a car standing at the curb. The engine started at once and the driver was away in a cloud of dust after the fire equipment.

"That's my style," said Mr. Joy and made an investigation of a similar model, found it to his liking and bought it on the spot. It was an 1899, single-cylinder Packard, built in Warren, Ohio. Eventually he interested a few friends in putting money into the Ohio plant, and it was moved to Detroit. Packard is one of the three surviving makes that began at the turn of the century—the others, Ford and Cadillac.

IT WAS A "DISTINCTION" TO BE ALLOWED TO CRANK A HORSELESS CARRIAGE, BUT A GOOD MANY AMBITIOUS VOLUNTEERS CARRIED THEIR ARMS IN SLINGS.

One of the first automobiles that Capt. Shuey, pioneer automobile dealer of South Bend, handled was the Long Distance Automobile, which "moniker," disillusioned owners claimed, was acquired because it could travel a longer distance from the blacksmith shop before it broke down than any other make. On another gas car the crank hung down in back like a sad dog's tail and in the course of a day's cranking made almost as many revolutions as the engine. Cap adroitly conveyed the idea that it was a distinction to be allowed to crank a horseless carriage, and a good many ambitious volunteers carried their arms in slings.

(Courtesy Diesel Div., General Motors Corp.)

WINTON WAS REALLY GOING TO TOWN WITH HIS ONE-CYLINDER CARS IN 1900. HERE
IS A PART OF HIS OUTPUT; THIRD FROM THE LEFT IS A SURREY (WITHOUT TOP).

STEAM CARS

One of the first steam cars to run, after a fashion, in this country was built by Ransom E. Olds in Lansing, in 1887. It was a three-wheeler, and two years later he built a four-wheel vehicle with vertical boiler, but with rare foresight turned his attention exclusively to gasoline cars and produced the famous curved-dash Oldsmobile which quickly made him a fortune. The Stanley Twins, who looked as alike as the famous cough-drop pair, Trade and Mark, brought out their first steamer in 1895 and in spite of a strict policy of no-paid-advertising their cars sold by the thousands and made them millionaires. Their only rival in this field was White, who built only three cars per week in 1901, and stepped up their annual output to 1,500 in 1906. In the following year they abandoned the steam car in favor of gasoline models. After two of the White contestants in one of the Glidden Tours burned up, this form of power lost its popularity.

CARTOON INSPIRED BY the author's first ride in a steam car in 1900. This is a Mobile Stanhope driven by Capt. Shuey, giving one of his famous sales talks. More of this unique character later.

1901 WHITE STEAMER

This is No. 260 made in the first year of automobile manufacture by the White Sewing Machine Co., of Cleveland. The boiler was a departure from those used in the Locomobile and Mobile, consisting of spiral coils of seamless tubing placed one above another in a casing of heat-resisting material. By an ingenious arrangement of connecting pipes the water entered the upper coils, while steam was generated in the intermediate coils and passed out of the lower ones next to the fire. There was no fixed water level to be maintained and no water gauge to be watched, the supply being automatically controlled by the steam pressure. This was known as the semi-flash type boiler.

Water tank capacity was 20 gallons. Later models were equipped with a condenser adding economy to the water supply. This condenser consisted of a number of horizontal tubes in a rectangular frame installed vertically in front, and from a distance looking very much like a Venetian blind. Note wicker basket behind seat, and folding buggy top.

(Courtesy Smithsonian Institution)

1900 LOCOMOBILE STEAMER

All of the American steam cars around 1900-1902 followed the general design of the first Stanley, in which the two-cylinder engine was installed vertically under the seat, the boiler under the rear deck with the water tank in U-shape around it.. The cylindrical boilers consisted of steel shells with some 300 copper fire tubes, the shells bound with piano wire. There were about 30 sq. ft. of heating surface, and normal steam pressure was 150 lbs., but could be run considerably higher than that, developing 10 to 12 brake horsepower for short periods. This was a relatively high ratio of horsepower to the 700 lbs. weight of the little car.

(Auto Club of Southern California Photo)

Note the light-weight chain and exposed sprocket, with a 16-to-40 tooth ratio from engine. Piston rods were only 5/16 in. in diameter. Gasoline tank was under floorboard. The first use of a rear-view mirror was applied to these steamers to enable the driver to see the water gauge at side of seat. Mirror was at side of right foot brake. Tires were 28 x 2 1/2" single tube with lugs cast in the rubber.

16

THE BEER BEGAN TO FOAM AND GREAT
BILLOWS SURGED OUT LIKE WASHDAY SUDS.

When Jimmy Studebaker opened up the Port of South Bend to motor navigation in 1899, the dog mortality increased about 300 per cent in his first week of cruising. The second week it dropped back to normal, but after that there wasn't any mortality; we ran out of dogs.

Jimmy created a lot of envy among the brown-derby patrons of Ireland's livery stable, which specialized in sleek trotters and red-wheeled, rubber - tired traps, and he had a monopoly on the public eye until Harry Stull bought a Mobile steamer. On short spurts these little animated teakettles could outrun the proverbial scared cat, and Harry had an annoying habit of slipping up behind Jimmy and shooting ahead like a guided missile.

This worked on Jimmy's ego until one day he found Harry's car parked outside Spring-brook ball park. At a roadhouse across the street a brewery truck was unloading kegs of beer. The water tanks of the Mobile held about a third of a barrel and were built around the boiler in back of the seat. Jimmy looked at the kegs speculatively and then at the Mo-bile's drain cock. He had a word with the grinning brewery driver and they busied them-selves about Stull's car a few minutes. Jimmy then drove down the road a piece to await results. In due time Harry came out and start-ed home. He didn't notice anything peculiar

for a while, but what with the sloshing and heat the beer began to foam and great billows surged out of the back like washday suds, and the fumes were well-nigh overpowering. It was said that respectable citizens began to weave all along the street and horses did everything but climb trees. People yelled at him but he had been yelled at before— mostly by kids and teamsters — and didn't pay any attention until, in making a turn, out of the corner of his eye he spied that billowing bubble - bath following him. He jammed on the brake and dove into the nearest saloon.

Jimmy, who had been trailing along to enjoy the fun, entered the saloon casually, and said, "Why, Harry, fancy meeting you here! After seeing you floating along in that fleecy cloud mass, I thought you'd gone to Heaven."

PUZZLED ABOUT HORSEPOWER?

Many persons are puzzled about the meaning of "horsepower." For example, if a twenty horsepower car gets stuck in the mud, how can one horse pull it out? Because the animal, for a short period, is exerting several times one horsepower, but he could not keep it up all day long. One horsepower is the equivalent of energy required to lift 33,000 lbs., one foot in one minute. By means of reduction gears one horse could do it, or a small one-horse-power engine could also.

FIRST STANLEY STEAMER

The first Stanley Steamer established a design which nearly all the other steam car builders followed, among them White, Toledo, Mobile, Locomobile, Stearns, etc. It consisted of a two-cylinder engine with cranks at 90 degrees, installed vertically under the seat with chain drive, the boiler under the rear deck with the water tank in horse-shoe shape around it. Later models of the Stanley had the engine installed horizontally, geared direct to the rear axle. Still later the boiler was placed under the hood. The Stanley twins built steam cars for over thirty years and in spite of not a cent spent on advertising, enjoyed a tremendous demand. Their latest model could not be distinguished from a gasoline car in appearance, although in action it was practically noiseless, and much smoother-running than any gasoline automobile.

(Brown Brothers Photo)

(Courtesy Smithsonian Institution)

RIKER ELECTRIC brougham of about 1900, now in the collection of the U. S. Museum, Washington, D. C.

COLUMBIA ELECTRIC Auto-
mobile, 1904. Part of the collection of the U. S. National Museum,
Washington, D. C.

IN THE EARLY days everyone who could
run the lathe had a go at building a car
of his own design, and some of them were
dillies. One prominent physician actually
installed cast iron gears in his transmission.

WILL WARNER had an appointment with
his banker one morning and set out to keep it,
in his Waverly electric. When he tried to
stop he discovered the controls were frozen
and had to keep going around the block until
the batteries ran down, much to the annoyance
of the banker.

RAUCH & LANG—1906

A handsome Rauch & Lang electric phaeton of 1906. They were the last word in elegance and comfort—but restricted to city and suburban use because of limited mileage, and costly batteries had to be renewed every two years on an average.

DETROIT ELECTRIC—1910

This is the 1910 Detroit Electric in which the author was badgered by the female members of the family into transporting a cat known to him privately as "Stinky," some potted

plants, table lamps and frilly lingerie on hangers from Pasadena to Long Beach when the family moved there for the summer. They had gone on ahead in the Hudson and left me to handle the more fragile boodle. The rolling showcase had just enough juice in it to make the thirty-mile trip, which wasn't so bad except

for the guffaws of passing truck drivers, and in one village a load of hay had toppled over, blocking the way which gave the gaping bystanders opportunity to display their wit.

"Better git that road cleared pronto," one local humorist called to the truckman," it's agin the law to hold up a hearse."

"Nice job of embalming," another put in, "corpse sure looks like it was alive. Sittin' up, too."

"No smell, noise, jolt, etc..."

STUDEBAKER ELECTRIC RUNABOUT

HUNDREDS OF THESE electric hansom cabs were in use in New York and other large cities in 1900, built by the Electric Vehicle Co. of Hartford, Connecticut. An electric motor drove each rear wheel, and thus no differential was required.

1901 OLDSMOBILE WITH DOS-A-DOS SEAT.

OLDSMOBILE

The little toboggan-dash Oldsmobile unquestionably was our most important motor vehicle at the turn of the century—the Dawn of Motordom in America. It was the first to be produced by assembly-line methods and 5,000 were turned out in 1904 while other makes were built only in hundreds.

Its popularity was well deserved for, coupled with its light weight of 700 lbs. and low price of $650, operation was extremely simple. You started it from the seat, an easy task because there was a 2-to-1 reduction by chain between crank and engine. There was one lever for the two forward speeds and reverse of its planetary transmission, a spark advance beside the seat, an accelerator under the right foot and a brake under the left. Practically all its simple mechanism was accessible by lifting up the rear deck.

But there was dissension between Ransom E. Olds and his partners in 1905 and production declined. They wanted to get into the higher price-class and Olds maintained their continued success lay in the original model which was selling so well. They would not compromise; result, Olds resigned to join the newly organized Reo company, named after his initials. Meanwhile the Oldsmobile engineers, after some expensive experimentation, produced a new model with no trace of its successful predecessor, having a detachable tonneau and "French type" hood concealing water and gas tanks. The engine was still under the seat. Its lines were pleasing for that period, but this model never appealed to the public as did the "Merry Oldsmobile" of Gus Edwards' song hit. For one thing, it was rather heavy for its horsepower.

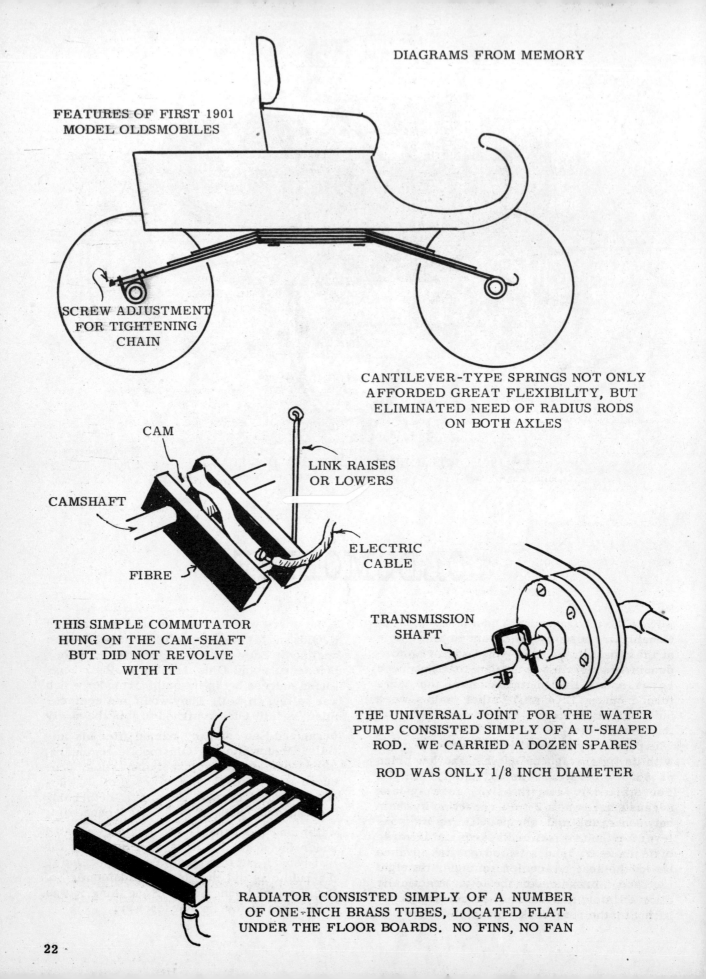

FEATURES OF FIRST 1901
MODEL OLDSMOBILES

SCREW ADJUSTMENT
FOR TIGHTENING
CHAIN

CANTILEVER-TYPE SPRINGS NOT ONLY
AFFORDED GREAT FLEXIBILITY, BUT
ELIMINATED NEED OF RADIUS RODS
ON BOTH AXLES

CAM

CAMSHAFT

FIBRE

LINK RAISES
OR LOWERS

ELECTRIC
CABLE

THIS SIMPLE COMMUTATOR
HUNG ON THE CAM-SHAFT
BUT DID NOT REVOLVE
WITH IT

TRANSMISSION
SHAFT

THE UNIVERSAL JOINT FOR THE WATER
PUMP CONSISTED SIMPLY OF A U-SHAPED
ROD. WE CARRIED A DOZEN SPARES

ROD WAS ONLY 1/8 INCH DIAMETER

RADIATOR CONSISTED SIMPLY OF A NUMBER
OF ONE-INCH BRASS TUBES, LOCATED FLAT
UNDER THE FLOOR BOARDS. NO FINS, NO FAN

"MERRY OLDSMOBILE" FEATURED IN GUS EDWARDS' POPULAR SONG HIT.

Here is the Merry Oldsmobile of 1902-1905 which won fame not only through its dependable performance, but on the publicity of Gus Edwards' song hit, "In My Merry Oldsmobile." Its single cylinder was rated at 4 1/2 h.p., it weighed 700 lbs. and sold for $650 without extras. Operation was very simple; the driver put his right heel on a compression-release pedal (hidden by the curtain below seat), turned on switch and cranked from the seat, the sight-feed oiler on the engine having been turned on by the small lever just below the center of the seat cushion.

To the right of this was a small knob for regulating the gas mixture, and just inside the right of the seat, not visible, was a spark advance lever. After the engine was started, it was speeded up by the pedal under the right foot, then the transmission lever at driver's right (here in reverse position) was pushed forward into low, then on to high. Note oil carriage lamps, not standard equipment. The first Oldsmobiles sold included one small bicycle lamp, operating on acetylene gas.

First directors' meeting of the Olds Motor Vehicle Company in Lansing, Michigan, August 21, 1897. The gentlemen were a bit cautious about aiming too high; R. E. Olds, manager, was "authorized to build one perfect carriage" (here the "perfect" is crossed out) "in as perfect a manner as possible" and later Sec. Stebbins inserted the "nearly" perfect. Subsequent events proved that designer Olds lived up to instructions, for the little curved dash Oldsmobile was darned near perfect for that era.

OLDSMOBILE 1905

1905 model brought out by the Oldsmobile Company after R. E. Olds resigned and joined the Reo organization. It had a 10 h.p. single-cylinder engine under the seat, but in spite of its European lines and "French hood," it did not meet with near the popularity of its curved-dash predecessor.

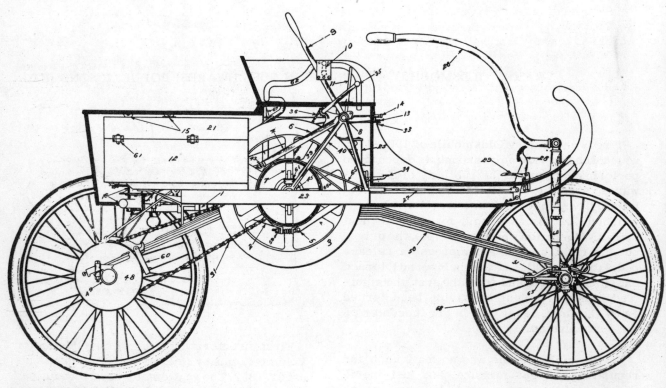

1901 OLDSMOBILE

Transverse section through the 1901 Oldsmobile, showing parts not visible in the top view. The following are listed in the order they would be used in starting: Switch 10, Oil Turn-On 13, Choke 14, Compression Release 34, Hand Crank 35, Foot Throttle 29, Low Gear Lever (same as for high and reverse), Foot Brake Pedal 28, Emergency Brake Lever 62.

Among other parts, Gas Tank 12, Water Tank 21, Filler Caps 15, Carburetor 16, Dry Cell Batteries 25, Tiller 26, Friction Clutch Spider Arm 7, Flywheel 3, Drive Chain 31.

WHEREVER THE Merry Oldsmobile stopped a crowd was sure to collect, asking all sorts of questions which the owner, proud of his automobile, answered willingly in detail. On one occasion a bystander said: "Mean to tell me they's four horsepower in that little buggy? Tain't safe — supposin' the thing gits completely out of control?"

AT RIGHT, BILL OF SALE for Olds which author's father bought in 1901.

<table>
<tr><td colspan="2">RALPH TEMPLE.
Pres. and Gen'l. Mgr.</td><td>TELEPHONE HARRISON 2033.</td><td colspan="2">CABLE ADDRESS
TEMPLE-CHICAGO.</td></tr>
<tr><td></td><td colspan="4">RALPH TEMPLE CO.
293-295 WABASH AVE.
CHICAGO, U. S. A., Nov 11 1901
SOLD TO A. P. Silvis
South Bend, Ind.</td></tr>
<tr><td>TERMS</td><td></td><td colspan="3">AUTOMOBILES, BICYCLES, BIKE WAGONS,
MOTOR CYCLES.</td></tr>
<tr><td>SHIPPED BY</td><td></td><td></td><td></td><td></td></tr>
</table>

Oldsmobile with top, doors, rear seat, side curtains, storm boot, storm apron — 685.00 — Received payment, RALPH TEMPLE CYCLE CO.

RAMBLER — 1900-1901

Charles T. Jeffery in the first experimental Rambler of 1900-1901. This is Model "A," its two-cylinder vertical engine under the hood a radical departure from the usual practice of that period, when most American engines were located under the seat. This also had a steering wheel, one of the very first, and left hand drive. It was designed by Charles T., but his father, Thomas B. Jeffery, founder of the Rambler, thought it too radical, and their first commercial passenger cars had the motors below the seat.

Charles T. Jeffery, incidentally, was a survivor of the Lusitania, having been picked up by a trawler after four hours in the icy waters off Ireland.

ENGINE OF THE Model "B" Rambler, also a two-cylinder vertical and mounted crosswise under the hood, had a flywheel at each end of the crankcase.

A. L. DYKE AN AUTOMOBILE PIONEER

This volume would not be complete without reference to some of the activities of A. L. Dyke, who can truly lay claim to the title of pioneer. Mr. Dyke's spark of interest began to glow when he watched his pioneer friend George P. Dorris start building his first automobile in 1895.

First Automobile Parts & Supply Business

A. L. Dyke's active interest started when he organized the first automobile parts and supply business in America in 1899, at which time a catalog of 32 pages with 50 illustrations was prepared and published early in 1900.

"All Dyked-Up"

In the early days when cars came bare of all accessories, it was the custom to go to Dyke's, or order from his catalog accessories, such as highly polished brass lamps, horn, etc. After equipping the car the motorist, as a rule, would purchase the conventional attire consisting of a pongee silk duster, gauntlets, goggles, and cap. To look and feel like a full fledged motorist he would then probably acquire a leather coat, trousers and leggings. He was then literally "all Dyked-up," hence the origin of that expression.

Dr. Dyke (Motor Doctor)

Mr. Dyke was also a pioneer publisher of automobile books. In 1903 he published "Diseases of a Gasoline Automobile and How to Cure Them." When a leading automobile magazine reviewed this book in its columns, it bestowed the title of M. D. (motor doctor). This proved to be a great advertising asset and "goodwill" for the A. L. Dyke Automobile Supply Co., who made caricatures of the old doctor in every conceivable manner, and used a slogan, "Dr. Dyke's Painless Prices." The old doctor at that time became very popular from coast to coast; in fact, in many parts of the world. In 1904 "Dr. Dyke's Anatomy of the Automobile" was published. This book contained 742 pages and approximately 350 illustrations. Many "first" cars appeared in this book, for example, the first curved dash Oldsmobile, first Model A Cadillac, first Ford with the opposed two-cylinder engine and planetary transmission, and others.

Dyke's No. 1 Outfit

The idea of supplying an outfit ready to assemble an automobile was originated by A. L. Dyke in 1899. It was known as "Dyke's No. 1 Outfit," and consisted of engine, transmission (sliding gear type), axles, wheels, steering device, radiator, etc., or in other words, the chassis less the body, which the purchaser could put together himself. This was very popular from 1899 through 1904. This outfit was sold to a great many experimenters who had an idea that they could build a better machine, and it was sold to others who just liked the idea of building their own car. It was necessary that Dyke build every part of this outfit. To those who have access to some of the early automobile magazines, which no doubt can be found in some of the libraries, we call attention to: The Motor Vehicle Review of May 15, 1900, pages 21-23 under "A Large Assortment of Parts," and in the Sept. 6, 1900 issue of the same magazine on pages 6 and 7, under "Oldest Motor Vehicle Supply House in America."

Automobile Manufacturer

A. L. Dyke was also a pioneer automobile manufacturer. In 1899 he organized the St. Louis Electric Automobile Company and built the "Dyke" electric; a runabout and stanhope. See Motor Age, May 10, 1900, page 284, also The Motor Vehicle Review, May 8, 1900, pages 27, 28. The assets of this company were sold in 1901 to The Scott Automobile Co. In 1903 the Dyke-Britton four cylinder gasoline, double chain driven car, with a combination four-in-one body, was put on the market, and in 1906 the DLG (Dyke, Leibert and Givens) six cylinder car made its appearance. This car was fully described and illustrated in The Automobile of July 18, 1907, on page 105.

A SINGLE-CYLINDER Winton of 1901. This had an enormous flywheel, and the "cooler" was a water tank in back with air flues through it. No radiator in front. Speed 20 m.p.h.

Dyke's Float-Feed Carburetor

As far as can be ascertained, the Dyke float-feed carburetor was the first American-made float-feed carburetor placed on the market (1900) to be used on any and all makes of gasoline engines. It was designed by A. L. Dyke and George P. Dorris. One of these carburetors is exhibited and preserved by the Smithsonian Institution, United States National Muesum, Washington, D. C. A similar carburetor is also preserved and displayed by the Museum of Science and Industry, Jackson Park, Chicago, Illinois.

Dyke's Auto Encyclopedia

Later, Mr. Dyke became the editor of the internationally known "Dyke's Automobile and Gasoline Engine Encyclopedia"; a book that could be termed a complete course of fundamentals in auto mechanics, the latest edition of which is available from the publishers of this book.

GEORGE P. DORRIS
AN AUTOMOBILE PIONEER

George Preston Dorris started on his first gasoline automobile in 1895. It was completed by 1897 and performed well, considering the fact that he had to design and make practically every part. In 1898 Dorris and associates organized the St. Louis Motor Carriage Company and built the "St. Louis" car until 1905. This car made quite a reputation for dependability. Its power plant was the first true

IN 1902 A STEERING wheel was adopted by the Rambler and louvres in the sides. Braking is on the wheels instead of differential, as in its predecessor.

unit-power-plant; with the sliding gear transmission submerged in oil in the crankcase of the horizontal single cylinder gasoline engine. In 1905 the Dorris Motor Car Company was organized, and with a modern well equipped factory they built the "Dorris" car until 1926; first a four-cylinder valve-in-head car, then a six-cylinder Dorris "Six-80" with an improved and patented distillator. This car won the economy record from Los Angeles to Yosemite Valley (Camp Curry) for cars of its weight and class for three consecutive years; 1920, 1921, 1922. Dorris is now engaged in business with his two sons building the Dorris speed reducers.

IN EARLY YEARS Packard engineers designed this first four-cylinder, but only a few
were built. It is Model K, with a distinctly
French flavor, engine under hood with radiator
exposed below in front. It appeared in 1903,
sold for $7,500!

(Courtesy Packard Motor Car Co.)

PACKARD 1900

NOW THE PACKARD has wheel steering.
This is a one-cylinder Model B, 1900, built
in Detroit. It is about to be tested by Chief
Engineer G. A. Hatcher, on New York to
Buffalo run.

THE LATE Frank Mayr, Sr., was among the
pioneers with a two-seated Milwaukee steamer.
It was a nice-looking horseless carriage with
a surrey body and almost noiseless in operation. It behaved reasonably well until some
slicker sold Frank a draft-inducer. The first
time he tried it the flame shot out the back
about two feet, which was all right as long
as he kept in the fairway, but once—and this
is legend—he backed up on old Doc Hool, a
local character of much facial foliage, and
burned off a considerable acreage of standing
crop. Doc was pretty sore, especially between
the chin and collar band, but didn't sue Frank
because he couldn't decide between a charge
of malicious trespassing or deforestation.

SPECIAL CAR BUILT BY JAMES WARD PACKARD FOR HIS PERSONAL USE, IN 1903.

JAMES WARD PACKARD in a special car he had built for his personal use in 1903, a one-cylinder of 10-12 h. p. His first automobile was a Winton, but he found so many things about it not to his liking that he took Alexander Winton to task. "All right," retorted Winton, "if you think you can make a better car, go ahead and do it." The reader may draw his own conclusions.

TOM FETCH HAD rugged going on his transcontinental trip from San Francisco to New York in this one-cylinder Packard of 12 h.p. He and mechanic were sixty-one days on the road, arriving in New York August 21, 1903.

FIRST TIRES

The first tires had smooth treads, relatively small section and large diameters (an Oldsmobile of 1910 had 42 in. wheels!) and carried up to 60 lbs. pressure. Original tires on the 1901 wire-wheel Olds were single tube, as on a bicycle, and held to the rim with small lugs cast in the rubber, After becoming somewhat worn a mastic filler was pumped into tires to render them puncture-proof. Standing on a hot day, being filled with a glutinous mass and not inflated, they had a tendency to flatten and remain in that condition until run several miles. When a mastic-filled tire burst, the jelly spurted into the air and congealed in thin shreds, looking as though a feather mattress had exploded.

FILLING STATIONS 1912

Filling stations didn't appear until the cars were fairly numerous, say around 1912, when there were 356,000 cars produced. At first we chugged over to the corner grocery for our gas for which we paid 9¢ a gallon. And it was good volatile gas, too, which we brought home in a can with a potato stuck on the spout. Four or five gallons were more than we could use in a day. Tanks for storage at home were put out by the Bowser Company, and we could keep a reserve of 50 gallons or more. A pump was included in the outfit.

A BATTLE-CREEK genius designed a horseless carriage body with a life-size horse's head in front to reassure its brothers on the road, but it deceived no steed because the sounds emanating from beneath the vehicle in no way resembled the most thorough-going abdominal rumblings of a hay burner.

WHITE STEAM SPORTSMAN runabout, with huge acetylene headlamps
and a rear deck that could double for a ski run. The bulb horn on the
left side of the seat seems to be out of reach for the driver, David Sowers.

AUTOCAR 1901

This 1901 Autocar is believed to be the first shaft-driven automobile built in this country. It had a two-cylinder water-cooled engine mounted under the hood. Note rear entrance tonneau with no door. Steering by crank, with gearshift lever just below, and at right is handle that operates the clutch. It is one of the first left-hand drive cars. It gave a very good account of itself on a trip from Ardmore, Pennsylvania, to the auto show in New York City on December 11, 1901, covering the frozen, rutty country roads in six hours.

ELECTRIC RUNABOUT.

STUDEBAKER AUTOMOBILES

"The Automobile with a Reputation Behind It."

WE are prepared to meet the needs of those who are seeking an automobile for convenient local use—a machine which can safely and easily be handled by any member of the family—or a full-powered tonneau car for wide radius touring

THE STUDEBAKER ELECTRIC

is equipped with Exide or Edison Batteries, and has been thoroughly tested by years of actual use. Made on lines of the Runabout, Victoria Phaeton, Stanhope, Surrey or Delivery and Truck Wagon (first two styles illustrated here). *The most convenient vehicle for physicians' use.*

THE STUDEBAKER TOURING CAR

A light, but powerful, Gasoline Tonneau Car, embodying the latest improvements in construction and sold at a fair price. Built by a firm whose reputation is a guarantee of thorough workmanship. Write for catalogue to

STUDEBAKER BROS. MFG. CO., Automobile Department SOUTH BEND, IND.

NEW YORK CITY, Broadway, corner 48th Street.
CHICAGO, ILL. : 378-388 Wabash Avenue.
KANSAS CITY, MO. : 810-814 Walnut Street.
SAN FRANCISCO, CAL. : Cor. Market and 10th Streets

PORTLAND, ORE. : 330-331 East Morrison Street.
DENVER, COL. : Corner 15th and Blake Streets.
SALT LAKE CITY, UTAH : 157-159 State Street.
DALLAS, TEX. : 317-319 Elm Street.

Branch Houses and Agencies in Other Principal Cities.

ELECTRIC
VICTORIA PHAETON.

from LIFE, 1904

Engines, Seats Everywhere

Engines, as well as seats, were hung here, there and everywhere. The Orient Buckboard of 1904 had one mounted on the rear axle, the little Crestmobile on the front dash; Adams-Farwell was driven by a rotary engine with five radial cylinders revolving in a horizontal plane under the rear deck; first Franklin engines were placed crosswise under the hood with upright, air-cooled cylinders. First American car to have an engine under the hood was the Pope-Columbia designed by Hiram P. Maxim in 1898. Cylinders of the Knox were air-cooled by radiation from hundreds of threaded studs screwed into the walls.

Do you find these in your Tool Box?

"Here is the kit of tools I carried in an old alligator bag of ample proportions," writes George M. Studebaker, Jr. "This kit was transferred to whatever car I drove and quite frequently I took it along in friends' cars. These tools were ALL used and many times I wished for more."

1 set of ten end wrenches
1 large monkey wrench
1 small monkey wrench
1 large pipe wrench
1 medium pipe wrench
1 small pipe wrench
1 ball-peen hammer, heavy
1 ball-peen hammer, light
1 riveting hammer
1 set of four cold chisels
1 set of three cape chisels
6 punches, assorted
1 center punch
3 pairs pliers
1 pair Bernard side cutting pliers
1 pair lineman's pliers
1 pair long nose pliers
1 cotter key puller
8 files, flat, round, three-cornered, half-round, assorted sizes
3 spanner wrenches
2 tire irons
1 hacksaw and blades
1 small portable vise
1 bearing scraper
1 claw hammer

1 short wrecking bar
1 soldering iron
1 small blowtorch
solder and flux
valve-grinding compound
resin (for slipping clutch)
friction tape
box of assorted nuts, bolts, lock, washers, screws and springs
box cotter pins
sand paper, emery cloth
box rivets
sparkplug terminals

primary wire
secondary wire
water pump packing
tire valves and caps
small bundle baling wire
extra links for drive chain
extra Prestolite wrenches
gas tips for headlights
canvas gloves
overalls
mechanics' soap

Additional equipment carried on Mr. Studebaker's current car included:

Rope for winding around tire to get out of mud, extra can of carbide, can of cup grease, fan belt, oil can, oil gun of syringe type, folding canvas water bucket, funnel, chamois for straining gasoline, plenty of cotton waste and rags.

THIS 1904 PACKARD WAS THE FIRST TO HAVE THE DISTINCTIVE RADIATOR OUTLINE.

EUROPEAN VEHICLES

In 1902-1903 European vehicles were far in advance of the American in design and performance; most of them were models of fine handwork and attention to detail. Up to 1905 there were more cars in Great Britain alone than in the United States. But if workmanship abroad was of a better quality, the ingenious Yankee inventor tended to get down to fundamentals and simplify construction. Also, absence of good roads made it imperative to build the cars stronger.

All through the experimental stage there was a wide diversity of body design—if indeed it could be called such—and application of power. Standardization of any feature was far in the future. Perhaps that is why the machines were so interesting. Having seen one car of today, you have seen them all. But not so then. A parking lot attendant would have gone berserk, because no two makes handled alike, or anything near alike.

FOUR CYLINDER BERG, built in New Jersey about 1902-1903 was one of first of American manufacture designed along European lines. This was owned by the late Col. George M. Studebaker, former head of the auto corporation. Note rack for luggage on top.

34

AN EARLY POPE-TOLEDO with Cape Top over the tonneau. Note wicker basket for walking sticks and umbrellas attached to the dash, the crank through radiator and the very long hub caps. This outfit could use a tire cover.

"I WON'T TAKE LESS'N 75¢"

John Ellsworth caused a good many sighs of yearning when he rolled by in his foreign-looking Berg, which had a handful of speeds and just about enough clearance to pass over its own shadow without an abrasion. Once on a tour in 1902 he ran over a chicken hen and, being a conscientious motorist, turned back to settle with its owner.

"Wall, sir," growled the farmer, "you shore have done it now. That was a prize hen."

"I'm mighty sorry," said John, "what do you consider her worth?"

The bereaved ignored the question and elaborated at great length upon the rare pedigree of the fowl, on the inability to replace her, and the fact that she was a family pet on top if at all. Two or three times John interrupted with an inquiry about the amount of damages, but the rustic continued his eulogy. John wondered if he had enough cash with him, and thought it would have been cheaper if he had run over a farm hand instead. Finally in desperation he demanded:

776339

"Well, I've got to go on. Give me an idea of what you expect so that I can make arrangements for a settlement. What's the best you can do?"

The farmer regarded him shrewdly for a moment and then snapped: "I won't take a penny less'n seventy-five cents."

THIS TWO-CYLINDER 1902 French Dar-racq looks almost like a toy. The engine was mounted vertically under the hood and the radiator hung just forward of the rear axle.

YOU THINK YOU HAVE TIRE TROUBLE TODAY?

Listen to this: Clincher tires, before the advent of the demountable rim, were tough ones to fix -- especially when they became literally welded to the rim with rust.

George M. Studebaker, Jr., in an experience of this kind had to borrow a fence rail and use it as a battering ram to loosen the tire. But it was no use. Then he used a hacksaw to cut it away; all went well until he reached the stranded piano-wire cable in the bead. One after another the hacksaw blades broke, but the last one finally fought its way through.

That was but half the job. Now for putting on a new tire without pinching the inner tube, forcing the obstinate casing over the rim, prying and straining with tire irons, skinning knuckles. Then up and down with the hand pump, up and down until your back began to break. Remember, those old tires carried sixty pounds! Many a good man dropped from heart failure on this job.

Few motorists today have but a vague idea of how tires are repaired. They drive com-fortably into a service station and by the time they have bought a package of cigarettes and studied a road map, their car is ready for the highway again.

STEERING CAME FIRST

A 104 page book on HOW TO DRIVE AN AUTOMOBILE published in 1908 stresses this point: "Steering. Steering is one of the first things to be learned by the novice, many good instructors insisting on its being the very first, telling the would-be driver to learn to steer before attempting to learn even the most fundamental things about controlling the power plant." It was written by one Victor Lougheed, said to be founder of the Lockheed airplane company, and who had so changed his name because so few persons could pronounce "Lougheed" correctly.

GEORGE STUDEBAKER, JR. BORROWS A FENCE RAIL AND USES IT AS A BATTERING RAM

(Brainard Dewey Photo)

WAS A TIME WHEN MOTORING WAS SHEER PLEASURE, AS WITNESS THIS SMILING GROUP. THE CAR IS A 1904 FRENCH DARRACQ, WITH HANDSOME OVAL HEADLIGHTS. NOTE COMMUTATOR ON FRONT.

ALEXANDER WINTON, the automotive pioneer, standing beside the rear wheel of his 1904 Model, with a big two-cylinder engine. The author well remembers the power-ful-sounding exhaust that went "Ka-HUNK, Ka-HUNK, Ka-HUNK" when it was idling.

Doctors Were Hopefuls

At the turn of the century there were a great many doctors among the hopefuls who went in for horseless carriages. Some were bona fide practicing physicians and others merely titular, though all became doctors of philosophy in the end. Perhaps the urge to experiment with unfamiliar anatomies led them on, but one and all soon discovered that the healing element of Mother Nature never assisted toward recovery in a motor affliction.

Dr. Myers' first experience was with one of those spindly, high-wheeled Holsmans, which Louis Nickel innocently referred to as a "Wholesome" but that was an incorrect classification. It had almost enough clearance to straddle a load of hay. The two-cylinder, air-cooled motor was slung beneath the body and it is said that on cold mornings the busy doctor built a fire under it, after the manner of stimulating reluctant mules. Transmission was accomplished by means of a pair of raw-hide cord belts running in sheaves on jackshaft and rear wheels and speed control was through varying tension of these belts. Sometimes,

on going down with belts too slack they would slip off and the driver would be none the wiser until he attempted the next grade.

"Doc" Williams was our designing genius and eventually turned out some creditable work. But his first creation, about 1906 or '07, had peculiarities. It had a huge four-cylinder double-opposed engine, and he named it the "White Ghost." Under his vigilant eye and virile language the hybrid car circulated intermittently, but it balked entirely in alien hands. About the time he decided to use it for a hen coop a religious sect in Benton Harbor decreed it sinful for any of their flock to use domestic or jungle animals as beasts of burden and Doc persuaded them to buy the White Ghost. Somehow he managed to get it the forty miles to Benton Harbor under its own power, but when the White Ghost met up with the long-haired prophets it gave a tired sigh and expired on the spot. Faith healing failed to resurrect it and the White Ghost became a permanent haunt in the vicinity of Benton Harbor.

ONE OF THE SIXTY-ODD makes of electric automobiles built in this country prior to 1915. Drive was through large enclosed spur gears on each rear wheel.

(Courtesy Auto Club of Southern California)

THIS FRENCH DARRACQ of 1904 was beautifully finished, with a great deal of fine handwork on the motor. Real leather was used for the upholstery and otherwise all materials were of the best.

(Courtesy of Brainard Dewey)

THE HIGH, WIDE and handsome "Holsman" could almost straddle a traffic cop, while the "Crestmobile" went to the other extreme and was designed to park under the porch.

The "Maxwell"

The Aristocrat of Moderate Priced Cars

MODEL L. D.
2-cyl. 14 H. P.
MAGNETO

THE ARISTOCRAT OF RUNABOUTS—$825

The logical car for business and pleasure. Completely equipped with Top—Gas Lamps—Generator and Magneto.

12,000 Satisfied Owners Prove Our Claims

that though moderate in price, Maxwell cars are made of as good material, with as careful workmanship under as rigid inspection, and are as durable as _should be_ the best high priced cars.

PRIDE OF

(Courtesy General Motors Corp.)

THE FIRST FOUR-CYLINDER Cadillac was a huge car, with hood extending well over the front axle, a practice to which designers have returned. It had a two-speed planetary transmission and enormous "artillery hubs" protruding so far that they nearly snagged the corner drugstore in making a turn. Not many were built.

(Courtesy Auto Club of Southern California)

(Courtesy Firestone)

POSSESSION PERSONIFIED

(Courtesy General Motors Corp.)

CONSARN THEM CITY DUDES!

THE FIRST CADILLAC OF 1903 HAD A ONE-CYLINDER, 10 H.P. ENGINE UNDER THE SEAT, AND BEING BUILT BY PRECISIONISTS LELAND-FAULCONER, IT WAS A GENEROUS TEN HORSEPOWER.

(Courtesy Dubuque, Iowa Chamber of Commerce)

THE ADAMS-FARWELL, made in Dubuque, Iowa, was unique with a five-cylinder rotary engine under the back seat. Cylinders revolved around a fixed crankshaft. They were air-cooled, with fins lengthwise, and supplying gas, oil and electricity to this whirling dervish required considerable ingenuity on the part of the driver.

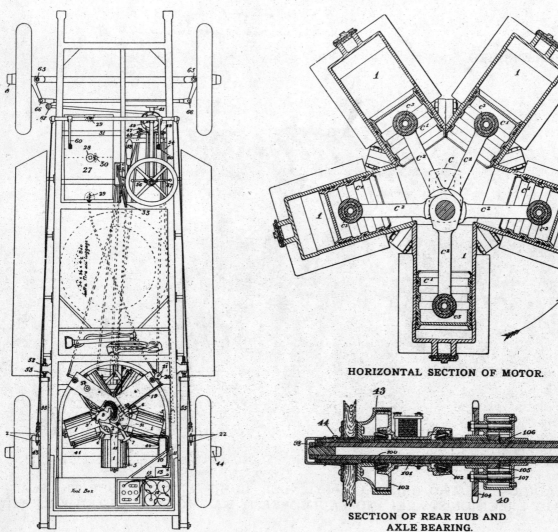

HORIZONTAL SECTION OF MOTOR.

SECTION OF REAR HUB AND AXLE BEARING.

Mechanical Features Adams-Farwell

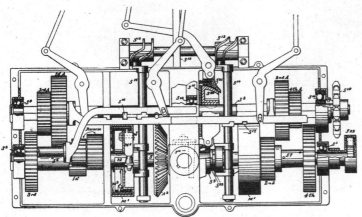

DOUBLE CLUTCH SLIDING GEAR TRANSMISSION.

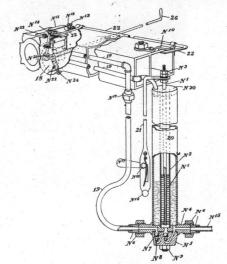

GASOLINE WELL. PUMP AND
CARBURETTOR.

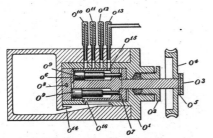

LUBRICATING OIL PUMP.

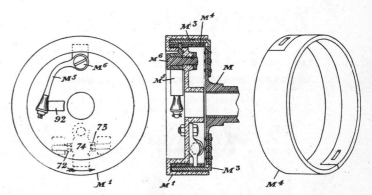

CLUTCH USED IN DOUBLE CLUTCH SLIDING GEAR TRANSMISSION

DESCRIPTION OF 1906 ADAMS-FARWELL:

The body was of the side entrance tonneau type, having individual front seats and extra roomy rear seat. Rear seat 52 in. wide inside. Color dark blue with light blue stripes or as desired. The wheel base 108 in. Tires: front 34 x 4 1/2, rear 34 x 4 1/2. Springs: front 40 x 2, rear 44 x 2 1/2. Brakes: internal and external band brakes on rear hubs. Frame: trussed angle steel. Total weight: 2,500 lbs. Horsepower: 40-45. Five cylinders, 5 in. bore, 5 in. stroke. Ignition: jump spark, storage battery or dry cells, automatic spark advance. Transmission: slide gear, double clutch, four speeds forward and reverse.

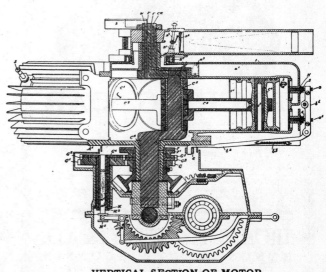

VERTICAL SECTION OF MOTOR.

(Courtesy Auto Club of Southern California)

TWO-CYLINDER RAMBLER OF 1907 HAD A TWO-SPEED PLANETARY TRANSMISSION, AND CRANKED FROM THE SIDE. NOTE HIGHLY POLISHED CARBIDE GAS TANK.

Walter Schneider of South Bend battled with an insistent Rambler in his own barn and barely escaped with his life. The barn was an old, weather-beaten structure on the side of a hill with a fifteen foot drop to the pasture below. Walter had, as so many of us absent-mindedly did, cranked the car in gear and promptly was pinned against the wall over-hanging the pasture. The clutch slipped just enough to prevent stalling the engine; meantime the ancient boards creaked ominously. Just as they seemed about to give way a neighbor, attracted by the frantic yelps, rushed in and snapped off the switch.

FOUR-CYLINDER RAMBLER OF 1908. THIS WAS FORERUNNER OF THE JEFFERY AND THEN THE NASH.

ON THE WAY TO THE DEPOT CHARLEY HIT A PILE OF DIRT AND CAT-APULTED THE BRIDAL PAIR HEADLONG ONTO THE PAVEMENT.

TWO OF THE best-known oldtimers in our town were the Frazier brothers, Charley and Joe. They were genial, unassuming boys who brought to the motor car business locally more popularity than some of the early models they represented. Charley was once a bicycle racer and with his handlebar mustache reminded one of pictures of Henri Fournier, the Frenchman who won the Paris - Madrid race in a Panhard.

Joe was an artist, all the way through, and once turned loose on a machine wouldn't eat or sleep until he had cured its ailment. He was a little fellow with a high voice. Town wags claimed that he used to be basso - profundo on the Machinists Quartette until he turned tenor from swallowing so much oil under the cranky cars he worked on.

The Fraziers at one time handled the Knox, an early model with a folding seat over the front axle, facing forward, and the boys did occasional taxi work. When the village belle was married the pair hired the Knox to take them to the depot. On the way Charley hit a pile of dirt in the dark and catapulted the bridal pair headlong onto the pavement. They spent their honeymoon in the hospital.

45

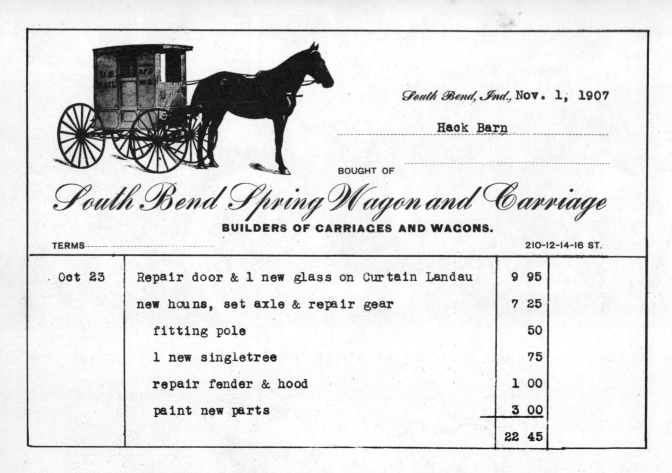

South Bend, Ind., Nov. 1, 1907

Hack Barn

BOUGHT OF

South Bend Spring Wagon and Carriage

BUILDERS OF CARRIAGES AND WAGONS.

TERMS

210-12-14-16 ST.

Oct 23	Repair door & 1 new glass on Curtain Landau	9	95
	new houns, set axle & repair gear	7	25
	fitting pole		50
	1 new singletree		75
	repair fender & hood	1	00
	paint new parts	3	00
		22	45

HERE'S THE BILL FOR REPAIRING A HORSE-DRAWN HACK
SMACKED INTO BY THE AUTHOR'S 1907 PERFECTION.

My own Perfection of 1907 had a curtain with a celluloid window for a windshield and crossing an intersection on a drizzly night

snapshot of the slightly damaged front of the car. This was my only accident in 49 years of driving.

the street light on the wet celluloid obscured my vision at the instant a horse-drawn hack crossed in front of me. At twenty miles an hour the damage was negligible, but it made a beautiful racket and was one of the first traffic accidents in South Bend. Here is a bill for repairs to the hack, $22.45, and a

TOP REMOVED to give it that "racy look." I liked to kid myself that it could attain the incredible speed of 25 m.p.h. but don't believe it ever went faster than 25. However, at that rate the roar and rattles made my passengers think we were going like hell. Color was blue with cream wheels—oh man!

46

"THEES AUTOMOBILE IS BALDINI, YES?"

Forty years ago scores of little shops all over the country assembled automobiles from engines built one place, transmissions another, etc., but bodies were usually turned out by local carriage makers. Frank Whitehall had one of these hybrids built by a man named Ricketts, who didn't think that was a very good selling name, so he went to the other extreme and called it the "Perfection," which didn't fit either, by a long shot. Somewhere Whitehall had picked up a nameplate with the inscription "Baldini, Torino" and had it brazed on to the radiator.

The author went with him to the Indianapolis races and arriving in that city drove into a garage for a minor repair. A mechanic, obviously a foreigner, asked what make of car it was and Whitey pointed to the name plate, whereupon the mechanic started to laugh.

"You say thees automobile is Baldini, yes?" he asked.

"Certainly," replied the owner, somewhat nettled.

"Mebbe so; I work for Baldini company in Italy before I come to thees country and he make the manure spreader."

ABOUT TO START out with confidence in 1907 Perfection. Note two bucket, or "rumble" seats.

Climbing a stiff grade into Berrien Springs, Michigan, the rear axle crystalized and parted, the car started backing down hill and barely missed running off the road into the river. This model was typical of the assembled car of 1905 to 1907. Motor, carburetor, transmission, axles and wheels all were manufactured in different places, and the mechanic could always make two parts fit with a file, chisel or sledge hammer. The wooden body was locally built.

RED BUG RACER WINS

AN EARLY ATTEMPT to sell junior autos. This was driven by an electric motor with two storage batteries. It was mounted on the same sort of chassis as the Orient Buckboard, a little car built at Waltham, Massachusetts, with a one-cylinder air-cooled engine mounted on the rear axle. It had two speeds but no reverse, and to turn around one had to lift up the front end and point it the other way.

HIGH SPOT OF the year was the annual trip to the Indianapolis Memorial Day race. Getting started at dawn, the 150 mile trip from South Bend took all day and we traveled through dust clouds of other cars the entire route. Here is our group to the 1912 event, left to right; the late Dr. Walter Baker, the author, Dr. Robert Shanklin and Frank Whitehall, owner, in the indispensable linen duster. This car is the "Baldini" of the anecdote.

IN THE EARLY days many gearshift arrangements differed from standard practice. One car (Dodge) in particular had the reverse in the position of first gear. A motorist driving up Mt. Wilson in one of these cars pulled in to one of the turn-out spaces to enjoy the view. When about to go on, he started the engine and shifted into what he thought was reverse, let in the clutch and plunged himself and passenger into the canyon below.

DR. STOLTZ, an able practitioner of generous displacement, chose a Crestmobile as a professional carrier. It was little more than a pneumatic-tired buggy on bicycle wheels with a tiny bicycle engine in front of the dash, and so small that he sat on it rather than in it. The doctor could start it from the seat by pulling on a strap wound around a pulley on the crankshaft, which automatically recoiled itself. Soon after he bought the machine "they say" he was working on a waterlogged customer out at Chain Lakes, and failing to get results after persistent pulling at the victim's tongue, absent mindedly muttered, "Hek— guess she's run out of gas again."

DR. HILL, a thrifty medico, enjoyed a cigar more than most and when making a professional call would lay his still-lighted stub on the car fender before entering the house. If he found the cigar out when he got back to the car he'd say, "Darn, I made that one too long."

A SOURDOUGH returned from Alaska with a rich poke in 1904 and settled down in Oakland to enjoy the luxuries of so-called civilization, but after years on his lonely mining claim, did not find them exactly to his liking. For one thing, eggs were too fresh, no kick to 'em. He liked them turned a bit. Then he bought an expensive automobile (said to be a Stevens-Duryea) and hired a chauffeur, but the car was temperamental and after one particularly exasperating tussle to get it started told his chauffeur to put it aboard the San Francisco ferry—"and when you get out to the middle of the bay, push it overboard." And that, according to a ferry passenger, is precisely what the chauffeur did.

SUCH NONCHALANCE IS achieved only with practice. One-cylinder Packard of fifty years ago.

REMEMBER THE BRUSH? Here's one of the relics of 1907—and it still runs. Operating on one cylinder, with "knee action" coil springs, carbide lamps, automatic clutch (just shift into forward or reverse and away she goes), this "runabout" was dug from a sand dune near Carson City and driven to Los Angeles recently by Cowboy Franklin Thompson, who is at the wheel. He is asking a Club touring bureau representative to look up the manufacturer who may have years ago inherited the Brush line of cars which originated in Detroit. He said this buggy was buried in sand and brush for at least fifteen years before he disinterred it. After replacing rotted tires and patching it here and there, he piloted the car 455 miles from Carson City to Hollywood.

ELLWOOD HAYNES
AND BICYCLE COP
IN CHICAGO, 1895.

First Endurance Run—1895

The year 1895 is especially significant because of the Chicago Times-Herald sponsored endurance run in Chicago, the first in America. The course was 53 1/2 miles from Jackson Park, up through Lincoln Park to Evanston and return west of the Loop to the starting point. Just before the start the Haynes-Apperson ran afoul of a streetcar and smashed a wheel, a collision that imposed a hardship on the motorman who had no language to cope with the novel situation. He and his brethren became more prolific of expression as automobiles increased in number. Another entry collided with a HORSE CAR near the Art Institute after the race was under way.

Of the four gas and two electric vehicles that started only two finished, the Duryea outspeeding an imported German Benz at an average rate of 5 1/4 miles an hour (elapsed time—running time about 7 1/2 m.p.h.). It was said that sand and resin had been applied to the leather belt drive of the Benz before it would take hold. The electrics dropped out early, unable to battle through a three-inch

snowfall on that epochal Thanksgiving Day and all of them wrapped rope around their tires to avoid skidding. Hiram Maxim, one of our most ingenious motor vehicle pioneers, was "umpire" on the Electrobat which was unable to cover the distance even though relays of freshly charged batteries were awaiting it along the route. Henry Ford wanted to attend the race but was unable to raise the money for his fare.

The now famous event caused so many runaways that the South Park Board in heated session next day ruled all motor vehicles off the boulevard system of the South Side, an edict that rather encouraged a practice among horsemen of driving alongside a motorist, lashing him with the whip and then trotting on. There was no comeback because none of the gas buggies could overtake a horse, unless it was lying down or sick. This year Hiram Maxim completed his motor-tricycle, having three air-cooled (theoretically cooled because the cylinders were smooth without fins) cylinders, four-cycle with electric ignition.

(Courtesy Smithsonian Institution)

ALEXANDER AT THE WHEEL of his "Bullet No. 1" racing car. This had a massive four-cylinder engine of 6 in. bore and 7 in. stroke, built in 1902. Winton did a great deal of racing and won many events, which publicity gave impetus to the demand for his passenger cars.

(Courtesy John T. McCutcheon)

THE IDIOT WHO STANDS OUT IN THE COURSE AT AN AUTOMOBILE RACE. (For further particulars see obituary column next Sunday.)

CROWN POINT ROAD RACES, ABOUT 1909.

BARNEY OLDFIELD BREAKS record for a mile lap in 55 seconds at Agriculture Park in Los Angeles, in 1903. Cars appear to be of same make, possibly two-cylinder Peerless. Race was a Good Roads benefit put on by Auto Club of Southern California.

CHALMERS "BLUE BIRD" at Crown Point, Indiana road races, 1908. Note nifty little circular windshield folded down on steering column. This was at finish of race.

THIS MASON WITH beetle-shaped body was driven by a four-cylinder motor with 4.316 bore by 6 in. stroke. Driven by Tower it is coming into the pits in the 1913 Indianapolis Speedway race. On the 51st lap it turned over.

A LOT OF ENGINE on four wheels in this Winton "Bullet No. 2." It was built for the fourth Gordon Bennett road race held in Ireland, 1903, and driven by Alexander Winton until a minor mechanical failure forced it to withdraw. In this car Oldfield covered a mile in 43 seconds at Daytona Beach, Florida, January 28, 1904. Power plant consists of two four-cylinder-in-line engines bolted together, with the cylinders lying horizontally. Bore was 5 1/2 in. by 6 in. stroke, and it had a total displacement of 1,029 in. Compare this with the 181.6 cu. in. displacement of a Miller-Hartz Special in the 1939 Indianapolis Speedway race, with a qualifying time of 124.125 m.p.h. Note small brake drums.

First Six Cylinder Engine in U.S.

CLAIMED BY the manufacturer to be the first six-cylinder engine developed in the United States, built by E. R. Thomas Motor Co., of Buffalo. It was rated at 60 h.p. and the price was $6,000. It was raced at Palm Beach in the winter of 1904-1905 by A. B. Shultz.

BARNEY OLDFIELD BEGAN holding a cigar in his mouth to prevent his teeth from biting his tongue while in a race. Invariably the cigar was unlighted. Note the mechanic with him in this Mercer racer—obviously a Frenchman. (The writer believes that this unidentified mechanic might be Gaston, brother of Louis Chevrolet.)

WAS THIS CARTOON of 1906 in Motoring and Boating prophetic?

BUICK RACER of about 1910 with Louis Nikrent at the wheel. His brother served as mechanician.

RAY HARROUN in the Marmon Wasp which won the first 500 mile Speedway race at Indianapolis in 1911. It was considered a sensational performance because he carried no mechanic, as did the other contestants. First money was $10,000.

(Courtesy Indianapolis Motor Speedway)

THIS IS THE once-famous Christy Front-Drive racer, in which the front wheels turned at the same speed as the engine crankshaft. It was said to be the very devil to manage, but that never daunted the indestructible Oldfield.

(Auto Club of Buffalo Photo)

ONE OF THE contestants in the 1912 Reliability Tour of the Auto Club of Buffalo was this Amplex "90," a huge well-built four-cylinder job. The engine operated on the two-cycle principle, which permitted it to turn counter-clockwise as well as clockwise with equal efficiency. The brake and gearshift levers were drilled, possibly to reduce the weight, but what about the mud? The driver is Roy Stains.

THIS PACKARD SPECIAL was built to test out airplane motor No. 399 at the beginning of World War I. Ralph DePalma is at the wheel. On our entrance into the war a larger engine, No. 999, was tried out in a car. This is illustrated below.

(Packard Motor Car Co. Photo)

(Courtesy Indianapolis Motor Speedway)

IN 1915 Ralph DePalma in a Mercedes won the 500 mile race, averaging 89.84 m.p.h. Breaking all previous records, winnings were $22,600. On the track DePalma often demonstrated fine sportsmanship. In the 1912 race, ten minutes before the end and he was conceded the winner, his Mercedes broke a piston. He and mechanic got out at once and pushed the car to the finish line. It was enough to crush the spirit of anyone but Ralph DePalma; he merely waved his hand at the grandstand and smiled.

(Pach Photo)

DE PALMA TESTS LIBERTY MOTORS

On July 26, 1918, Ralph DePalma was sworn in as an honorary captain of the New York Motor Police Corps during a police field day at Sheepshead Bay, when he gave a ten mile exhibition run with this Packard "999," built to test the forerunner of the Liberty airplane motor. The body was one of the first designed for scientific streamlining. On the front axle a tapered strip was secured to the rear edge with tape (faintly visible in photo) and painted over. Front ends of frames, radiator cap were streamlined, as were other parts where it was possible to do so.

OF NINE MODELS Sears-Roebuck had built under their name between 1905 and 1910, one was priced as low as $325. Quite a number of high-wheelers were manufactured in the early days to keep the machinery out of mud and dust and dirt.

(Auto Club of Southern California Photo)

ANOTHER HIGH-WHEEL-ER—a 1908 Firestone-Columbus. Note the buggy brake on the rear wheel.

DRAWN ESPECIALLY FOR THIS BOOK BY CLIFFORD McBRIDE,
CREATOR OF THE COMIC STRIP "NAPOLEON AND UNCLE ELBY."

ANECDOTES....

"NASHES TO NASHES"

Remember the catch phrases of the 'twenties? "Nashes to Nashes—Stutz to Stutz." The Scripps-Booth became the "Slips Loose," the Stoddard Dayton the "Stuttering Dago," the Holsman the "Un-Wholesome," and the good E. M. F. had several unflattering monikers, including "Every Man Fooled" and "Every Mechanical Failure."

MODEL "T" WAS NINTH

An informal quiz disclosed that actually there are persons who believe that Henry Ford, fed up with farm work, ran away from home and promptly invented the Model T and started getting rich at once. Fact of the matter is that he created eight different models, not including his first experimental car of 1906, before the famous "T," lost considerable money for himself and stockholders, made a lot of his associates angry through his stubbornness and didn't really get on his feet until he was forty.

"BUT DID YOU EVER SEE PLUM TREES LOOK SO BEAUTIFUL?"

Once my father was having a demonstration in a Mobile steam Stanhope and asked to be taken up Leeper's Hill, outside South Bend, which was long but not very steep. Halfway up the salesman, with a furtive eye on the steam gauge, slowed to a stop.

"Anything wrong?" asked father.
"Oh, no," replied the driver, indicating a blooming orchard on the side opposite the gauge, "but did you ever see plum trees look so beautiful?"

After a bit of conversational stalling steam rose to normal and they continued on to the top.

When the story got around, whenever a pioneer motorist failed to start his car, some kibitzer—and there were plenty of them in those days—was sure to remark, "Ever see plum trees look so beautiful?"

SPRAG

AL ABERNETHY, A FORMER VERMONTER, TELLS THIS ONE:

Bristol, Vermont, is on a sort of plateau and all roads out of town are down hill. Early day motorists thought twice before venturing beyond the relatively level streets of the town. But one citizen who owned a high - wheeled machine of modest power braved the hazards of the outer world by a special device. He fitted a sprag to the rear axle and a pair of tugs with a horse collar on the front axle. When starting the climb back up into town, he dropped the sprag, shifted to low gear, jumped out and putting head and shoulders in the horse collar pulled ahead while the little motor did its part. The combined effort was just enough to bring the vehicle over the hump into town.

HIGH-WHEELED Holsman of 1902, driven across continent in 1936 by J. H. Ozmun. Power was applied by swinging jackshaft forward, thus tightening the rawhide belts. To reverse, jackshaft was moved back, loosening belts and causing small pulley to rub against tire of rear wheel. This maneuver also served for braking. Air-cooled engine under body. On front axle are brackets for attaching shafts in case a horse is needed to tow it home.

1902 HOLSMAN CROSSES CONTINENT IN 1936

1906 PIERCE Great Arrow, owned by George Donald, Weston, Massachusetts.

DON'T LET that Packard type radiator fool you—it's a 1907 French De - Dion-Bouton. Owned by Agnest Lyons, Wakefield, Massachusetts. Car restored by Dean Fales, Professor of Automotive Engineering, at Massachusetts Institute of Technology.

(Photos Courtesy of Wallace Woodworth)

THESE TWO MEMBERS of the Packard test crew have mustaches trimmed after the manner of the great Henri Fournier, the French race driver, an idol of the period (1905 test car, on 1000 mile run).

(Packard Photo)

NOT UNTIL THE industry was firmly established were veils replaced by windshields, even on the most expensive cars, as witness this fine Packard touring car of 1909.

THE AMERICAN AMPLEX built in Mishawaka, Indiana, had a two-cycle engine, which type was capable of running counter-clockwise as well as the other way, and often did after a backfire. Milt Pine cranked his Amplex in the barn and in his hurry to get to the office overlooked a backfire; he shifted into reverse to back out of his barn and gunned the engine, then let in the clutch. The big machine shot through the back wall of the barn and fetched up against a neighbor's privy.

HANDSOME AND COSTLY STUDEBAKER OF 1907 WITH MAKE-AND-BREAK IGNITION, OIL SIDE LIGHTS, ACETYLENE HEADLIGHTS.

IT IS UNDERSTANDABLE that persons who could afford it bought European cars when you compare this luxurious 1908 Mercedes-Benz with any American automobile of that year.

IT IS REPORTED that a disgruntled purchaser of an early Winton drove his reluctant car behind a team of horses in Detroit, with a sign on it "THIS IS THE ONLY WAY YOU CAN DRIVE A WINTON." The Cleveland manufacturer then put a jackass in a farm wagon, hitched it to one of his cars and had the driver follow the dissatisfied customer. On the wagon was a huge sign "THIS IS THE ONLY ANIMAL UNABLE TO DRIVE A WINTON." Customer quickly faded out of the picture.

A LITTLE-KNOWN model, the "Michigan" of 1902-1903, with tiller steering.

BARNEY OLDFIELD in a Packard 1907 Sport Roadster before he started wearing cigars.

THE "MICHIGAN," first car put out by the Detroit Automobile Company, designed by Ford in 1901. Ford's experiments cost $86,000 and he was given an opportunity to resign.

(Packard Motor Car Co. Photo)

HENRY B. JOY, PRESIDENT OF PACKARD, AND HIS ASSOCIATE, RUSSELL A. ALGER IN A ROADSTER THAT WAS THE ENVY OF EVERY DRIVER OF A HUMBLE "ONE-LUNGER."

FORD MODEL B 1905

The Model B of 1905 was Ford's first four-cylinder job, a sweet-running, very quiet car for that period, with a two-speed planetary transmission. A departure from the tubular front axle on nearly all cars at that time is the I-beam section.

Dan Gise, a Hoosier motorist driving one of these, was superstitious about any of his passengers wearing a white necktie, (not the kind that goes with tails, however) which item of haberdashery was popular for summer wear in 1905. Sure enough, when he reluctantly consented to include the author wearing a snowy four-in-hand on a Sunday tour, the front axle parted exactly in the middle before we had gone ten miles. Even in this view can be seen the factory weld.

MODEL C FORD, 1905

(Edison Institute Photo)

This two-cylinder was popular and dependable, and did much to build the Ford reputation in the early days of motordom. Cylinders were opposed, horizontal. Note handy distributor below front seat. It was cranked from the right side.

FORDS, Model "C" and "N"

The famous Model T was two years in the future when Ford produced this four-cylinder Model N in 1906. L-head cylinders were cast in pairs with the heads integral, and to slip a pair over the pistons after scraping out carbon was a tricky job, inspiring some fancy language, as the author well knows from personal experience. A choke wire came out through the radiator, and the water pump was also outside, just below the crank. Like the Model T, it had a two-speed planetary transmission. Hood was one piece and tires 3 in. by 28 in. In heavy sand it used to hump up its back and shudder. But what a lot of fun!

MODEL K FORD 1906

(Edison Institute Photo)

A little-known Ford, the Model "K" of 1906-1907. It was a very fast six-cylinder job. On a visit to the Ford factory the author was given a ride in a test car driven by Frank Kulick, who did some racing for Ford. We sat on a soap box sketchily fastened to the bare chassis and when he opened her up out on Woodward Avenue, the sensation was just like dropping in a runaway elevator.

This was another car too expensive for profitable manufacture, the price about $2,750.

(Courtesy Better Homes and Gardens)

"EVER GOING TO GET THE THING STARTED? THESE EGGS ARE GETTING HEAVY."

"T" FORD out in 1908—NUFF SED

MODEL S FORD—1908. Here's a snappy little sport roadster with rumble seat for chauffeur in back and probably the model that inspired "the car with a rattle in front and a rumble behind." The sweeping fenders and running board were an innovation.

(George M. Studebaker, Jr. Photo)

THIS WELL - BUILT 1908 Studebaker is representative of the quality of workmanship that was characteristic of Studebaker from the beginning.

STUDEBAKER

South Bend youngsters of the 'nineties were used to seeing the smart turnouts of the Studebaker family, the traps, spider phaetons, coupes, broughams, landaulets. There was even a station wagon, and graceful victorias with their high-stepping horses and jingling martingales; but it was not until the company began to experiment with horseless vehicles that we sat up and took notice, following each new development from the first electric runabouts on up to the Flanders and E. M. F.

Once, in exchange for a ride in our curved-dash Oldsmobile I was permitted to drive — or try to drive — an experimental electric express wagon. It was a ponderous vehicle, with iron-tired wagon wheels and a ton of batteries hung below the body. It had a steering wheel, the first I'd ever had my hands on, and in trying to turn it out of the car tracks on west Washington street I nearly tipped it over. It was a pleasure to return to the steering tiller of the easily managed Oldsmobile.

YOU REMEMBER how the headlamps of the Model T Ford were set in forks well forward; a Texas rancher was driving along a narrow trail when he came upon one of his lanky steers standing in the road, hind end toward him. The critter disregarded his honking and continued to stand still, so the rancher thought he might stimulate the beast by bringing his hot radiator right up against his rear, which he proceeded to do. The steer came to life pronto and with a mighty two-legged kick lifted both lamps right out of their forks.

HUPMOBILE, 1910 VERSION

Hupmobile brought out a trim little runabout of 20 h.p. in 1908, with four cylinders and two-speed gearshift. Here is a 1910 version, same model owned by the author, who found it just about perfect transportation, light on its feet, quick pickup and easy to get in and out of. It sold for $750. Later a four-passenger model was built.

ALL SET FOR NIGHT DRIVING

The owner of this E. M. F. took no chances after nightfall, what with an acetylene tank on the running board and a Prestolite tank below. In the former, water dripping onto lumps of dry calcium carbide generated the gas, which was erratic in behavior. A big blob of water would suddenly create enormous pressure, and the rubber bag in the gas line would swell up like a "pizened pup." If the motorist didn't get around to the headlamps in a hurry they would fill with gas and when lighted invariably singe off eyebrows and mustache. After the gas was exhausted from the carbide a messy, gray, foul-smelling mass had to be dug out of the container. The Presto tank was easily controlled, a needle valve releasing the compressed gas as required. Empty tanks were exchanged.

(George M. Studebaker, Jr. Photo)

EARLY MODEL GARFORD, minus running board and apron, giving a full view of the novel muffler. Note splendid ventilation between top of tall windshield and front of top.

COMMEMORATIVE SERIES, 1901.

UNITED STATES

OF AMERICA

4   4

AUTOMOBILE

POSTAGE FOUR CENTS

REPRODUCTION OF THE commemorative four-cent stamp, with illustration of an electric brougham, issued during the Pan-American Exposition in San Francisco in 1915.

CHALMERS THIRTY, 1910. A very good car of this period. With racing body it gave a good account of itself at Crown Point, Indiana races of the period.

THIS FIRST Studebaker two-cylinder car of 1904 sold for $1,750, including detachable tonneau.

(George M. Studebaker, Jr. Photo)

SCENE ON a Glidden Tour. Crowd in background watching team of horses drag contestant out of the ditch. Packard official car at left; at right 1904 Franklin.

(Packard Motor Car Co. Photo)

BY REMOVING rear seat, this 1908 Studebaker Suburban served as baggage and passenger car, and with full-size seat, light touring car with folding top.

(Courtesy George M. Studebaker, Jr.)

First FRANKLIN SOLD

In the first Franklins, 1902-1904, the four-cylinder air-cooled engine was mounted cross-wise under the hood, driving through a long chain to the rear axle. The differential was not enclosed in a housing and on newly graded country roads, where it was the custom to scrape the dirt from the sides to the crown, the differential would drag and rocks between chain and sprocket would break the former. Intake valves were automatic; i.e., operated by suction rather than mechanically, and occasionally the nut on the stem would come off and the valve drop down into the cylinder with considerable racket ensuing. On a warm evening one could see the Franklin approaching by its red-hot exhaust pipes. The chassis sills were wood, and being of light construction throughout the car was lively and an excellent hill climber. Illustrated above is the third Franklin built and first one sold. It was rated at 7 h.p.; later models of this design developed 10 h.p.

THE FIRST CHEVROLET of 1912 retailed at $2,150, and the company was no threat to rival manufacturers until they entered the low price field. But look at them now!

CHEVROLET 1912

THIS EVER
HAPPEN
TO YOU?

Novel Vote for the Franklin

Enthusiast for the Air-Cooled Motor Gives Illustrations to Prove His Selection.

The following unique "Vote" was received this week for the Franklin Car in the competition for the best motor car:

THE BEST MOTOR CAR - I should say, is among gasoline machines, because the propelling mechanism is more simple and compact for the power developed than in steam cars. The cost of operation is also much less. Of all motors, those with the largest practical number of cylinders have the least vibration and the most flexible control. A four cylinder motor gives two impulses in each revolution, while a single cylinder gives only one impulse in two; hence the pull in a four cylinder is more continuous. A car equipped with same, is a better hill climber than one with fewer cylinders, because it has less opportunity to slow down between strokes. There are no unnecessary complications in the best motor car — The water-cooling system is unnecessary — a motor can be successfully cooled with air, while pipes, pump, radiator only add weight and require more or less attention — especially in winter. The motor is accessible under hood in front, while transmission is as simple as is practical, two speeds forward on one clutch lever; and direct drive by chain with no intermediate gearing, giving greatest efficiency of motor. The best motor car has ample power for its weight, secured by the light air-cooled motor. This enables car to take hills on the direct drive, saving time otherwise lost running on slower intermediate speeds and the trouble of changing gears. Yet motor is not geared so low on direct that best speed on the level is under 30 miles. The second speed is powerful enough for all emergencies. By virtue of this up-to-date construction, the best motor car will travel all sorts and conditions of roads in good time and in any weather —

Therefore the BEST MOTOR CAR is beyond doubt

THE FRANKLIN LIGHT TONNEAU.

By WAHRHEIT

At the beginning of this century there was a great deal of controversy as to what form of power, electricity, steam or gas would dominate the field in the future, and the gas adherents were divided between water and air cooling. The magazine Motoring and Boating, New York (long since extinct) ran an essay contest on the subject "The Best Motor Car" in 1906, but my vote for the Franklin, herewith, didn't get anywhere.

LOZIER (CIRCA 1908) with chauffeur's seat on running board.

SOME YEARS ago an enterprising adventurer from Texas wanted to come to Los Angeles the worst way (which was precisely the way he chose), but lacking cash for a railroad ticket scraped together the $10.00 or so needed to buy a discarded Ford, minus the engine. He persuaded a friend to tow him out of town to a lonely stretch of road, and there he waited. To the first motor Samaritan who drew up to assist our hero explained he simply could not get his car started which, being the truth, was fair enough. So the unsuspecting stranger towed him to the first repair shop. From that point our friend picked up another tow and by relays eventually got across the California state line.

"Pretty soft," he exulted—under his breath, of course. "I'll make the last stretch in one hop," whereupon he let his last victim haul past two or three repair shops. Naturally the latter became suspicious and stopped abruptly.

"Say, lemme see your engine," he demanded, and yanked off the hood. Then he loosed one straight-arm wallop, cut the tow rope and drove on.

(Courtesy of Tod Ford)

ANOTHER CAR with large wheels was the American Underslung, so called because the springs were hung under the axles, bringing the chassis close to the ground; and the manufacturers made special claim for safety because of low center of gravity. The wheels were 40 in., the engine 25 h.p. on this roadster. A 50 h.p. model was also built in 1910, which sold for $4,250. It was considered a very smart job at that time.

(Courtesy Auto Club of Southern California)

ONE OF THE EARLIER Detroit made cars called "the Northern." It was advertised as "the Silent Northern—Silent as the Stars." It was of the two-cylinder opposed type. The picture was taken in 1907, and the car was built in 1905.

IN THE DAYS of rear-entrance tonneaus one could back up to the curb on either side of the street and unload his passengers like he would a ton of coal. That thing on milady's head is not a basket of fruit being returned, but a hat—and, for that period, no exaggeration.

"LET'S GET TOGETHER," SAID A COUPLE OF PACKARD LIMOUSINES IN 1911.

WHEN THERE WAS only one car to each fifty persons, it naturally had to carry as many as could climb aboard. Thomas Flyer of 1906 owned by I. W. Gleason of Los Angeles. One plucked his food from trees, women lifted beehives for hats.

"I was going fifty?"

ONE OF THE first camp trailers, built especially for the late E. R. Tutt of Oakland, hauled by Packard Twin Six.

GERMAN PROTOS of the New York-Paris Race after undergoing repairs in South Bend.

NEW YORK—PARIS RACE 1908

On February 12, 1908, a Thomas Flyer, a French Moto-Bloc, a German Protos, a French Sizaire-Naudin, an Italian Zust and two French De Dions started from New York on a race to Paris, sponsored jointly by the New York Times and Le Matin. It was a tough time of year for any kind of motoring, let alone a 'round-the-world race, and the contestants fought terrific battles with snow, ice and mud right from the start. The author helped shovel the Thomas Flyer through the drifts from Elkhart to South Bend, Indiana, an all-night ordeal in which the American car covered only 14 miles. The other contestants were scattered all over the eastern part of the United States.

It is said that a well-equipped machine shop on wheels was not too far from the Thomas all the way. Before they reached Chicago the Moto-Bloc and Protos were practically dismantled in a repair garage in South Bend before they could be put in shape to continue the struggle.

After 42 days of incredibly rough going the Thomas was shipped to Alaska by boat with the idea of crossing the Bering Strait to Siberia over the ice. But there was no ice, and it had to turn back. In Seattle all the surviving contestants were put aboard ship for Vladivostock. Crossing Siberia was a nightmare; the Protos arrived in Paris four days ahead of the Thomas, but the American car was adjudged winner as in actual travel it was 26 days ahead in elapsed time. Having known how the American crew felt even before they reached Chicago, I'll wager none of them at the finish of the race even wanted to see an automobile for a long, long time.

FORERUNNER OF the camp trailer, this camp car mounted on a Packard Twin - Six chassis was built in 1915 for Henry B. Joy, and was considered a great advance in camping convenience, having canvas bunks, kitchenette, ice box, running water and ingenious drawers and compartments for miscellaneous equipment. The author made an overnight trip in it along the Mexican border during the Villa uprising. Mr. Joy proved an adept outdoor chef and we slept on the desert. In the middle of the night a couple of bullets whined overhead; we thought we were being ambushed by Mexicans. Mr. Joy reassured us: "They tell me that in the Battle of Juarez over two thousand shots were exchanged and only one goat killed. I think we're safe." Later we learned the shots were fired by a cowpoke on a binge.

On an earlier trip McCulla and the author were fired on in earnest, and the car damaged.

ON THE MEXICAN BORDER with the Packard camp car. Left to right: Henry B. Joy, Bill McCulla, E. C. Morton, and the author.

Hi Sibley's Pen Interprets Chicago Show Features

1915 STUTZ BEARCAT. Wilbur T. Dur-
borough, was correspondent in Villa campaign
on Mexican border, taken May, 1916.

FROM ABOUT 1908 to 1915 was the Age of
Brass. A proper car had almost as much
polished brass as paint, what with big Phare-
Solar headlamps, oil side and tail lamps,
windshield frame with long braces to the front
end of the chassis, rails around the tonneau,
door handles, hub caps and several feet of
flexible brass tube from speedometer on the
dash to a gear on the front wheel, another
for the brass bulb horn, and miscellaneous
brackets and things all over the place. Two
hours was the average time required to polish
all that effulgence on a Sunday morning.

WHEN EDWARD PAYSON WESTON, seven-
ty-year-old professional pedestrian of forty
years ago, walked 45 miles non-stop from
Ligionier, Indiana, to South Bend, he was paced
by an official car called the "Gearless Six"
which quite often was also motionless. Milk
and tea for Weston were kept hot on the
exhaust manifold.

HORACE KIZER, young man-about-town in
South Bend forty years ago, wore a Sherlock
Holmes cap and smoked a huge curved-stem
pipe as he roared around in his big Lozier,
muffler wide open. Once, starting away from
a ball park in a crowd, he bowled over an
early-day traffic cop. Confused by the yells of
bystanders he backed up and ran over the cop
again. It was soft ground and did no great in-
jury to the legs of the victim, who afterward
said he wouldn't have minded so much if only
Horace had used the same tracks on the
return trip.

TO PREVENT SPEEDING in Glencoe, Illinois, the city had ridges built across the
street at intersections and these became known
to all motorists as "Glencoe bumps."

HARRY C. STUTZ, designer of the famous Stutz Bearcat, in his first car, 1906.

First BUICK 1903

(Courtesy General Motors Corp.)

A VIEW of the first Buick of 1903 with its clothes off, obviously just after a road test. It was customary in those days to actually run the car over roads of varying conditions. This is a two-cylinder model, and you will see the water tank behind the radiator, instead of the engine. Tied on top of it appears to be an emergency oil can for the test run.

(Courtesy General Motors Corp.)

1907 BUICK MODEL "G"

Two-passenger, turtle back roadster, 89 in. wheelbase, two-cylinder engine with 16.2 h.p. Selling price F.O.B. Flint, Michigan, $1,150. Top was $70.00 extra. Tires 30 x 3 1/2.

1910 BUICK MODEL "10"

(Courtesy General Motors Corp.)

PRICE, F.O.B.—$1,050   WEIGHT—1,750

WHEELBASE—92   TREAD—56

ENGINE—4 cyl. 3¾ x 3¾ - 165.6 disp.
H.P.—Max. brake 18   S.A.E. 22.5
Valves—In head, removable cages.
Cooling—Water with pump.
Carburetor—Schebler.
Lubrication—Pump and splash.
Ignition—Remy magneto, Remy coil,
Vesta storage battery, set of dry
cells in reserve. Self starting
spark feature.
Engine mounting—Sub-frame.

CHASSIS—Frame—Pressed steel.
Springs—Semi-elliptic front, full
elliptic rear.

REAR AXLE—Bevel gear, torque tube.

TRANSMISSION—Planetary type. 2 speeds
forward and 1 reverse.

CLUTCH—Cone type with large area of
contact surface.

BRAKES—Service—External contracting on
transmission shaft.
Parking—Internal expanding on
rear wheel hubs.

STEERING—Semi-irreversible type.

WHEELS—Wood spoke. Clincher, Quick
Detachable, or Standard Universal
rims.

TIRES—30 x 3½

BODY—4 passenger tourabout type.
Finished in Buick grey.

MISCELLANEOUS—Upper and lower sections of
crankcase were cast of aluminum.
Standard equipment was oil lamps,
tail lamp, generator, gas headlights,
horn, and repair outfit. Prest-O-
Lite equipment was optional for gas
generator if desired. Total
production for the three types of
Model 10 was 11,000 cars.

(Courtesy General Motors Corp.)

FEW OLDTIMERS WILL RECOGNIZE THIS AS A BUICK, ONE OF A FEW EXPERIMENTAL
MODELS WITH A TWO-CYLINDER, TWO-CYCLE ENGINE HAVING 5 IN. BORE AND 5 IN.
STROKE. IT DEVELOPED 20 - 24 H.P. AND WEIGHT WAS 1,800 LBS. BUILT IN 1906.

WINDSHIELDS still had to be braced like billboards, as on this 1910 Buick. The top half folded over, giving the driver a breath of fresh air along with a lungful of gnats and an occasional ill-advised bumblebee.

ONE OF THE big thrills of my youth was riding down Broadway, New York, in one of these with a schoolmate at the wheel, conscious of the admiring glances of pedestrians (at the car, not the payload). This Simplex of 1912 was one of America's finest cars, double side-chain drive being used on the Locomobile and Thomas Flyer. The theory was that a stronger rear axle was possible, being fixed and with only the wheels revolving. The differential was on the jackshaft carrying the small sprockets.

AMERICAN AUTOMOBILES were the favorites in Japan from the beginning, due to interchangeability of parts and relatively low prices, although the large English colony naturally preferred British makes. Here is a 1916 Overland Country Club model belonging to Dick Andrews, an importer, at the wheel.

For country touring this was preferred to his Cadillac because the short wheel base enabled it to make right-angle turns on the very narrow country roads, many of them on the top of dikes between rice paddies. This snapshot taken en route on a picnic trip to Mt. Fuji.

Here's WHERE We Got Started—

1893. The Duryea brothers, Charles E. and J. Franklin build and operate a one-cylinder horseless carriage in Springfield, Massachusetts, said to be the first in America, with gasoline power. It was the first with electric ignition and spray-type carburetor.

1894. Elwood Haynes of Kokomo, Indiana, designs a one-cylinder gasoline carriage built by the Appersons, Elmer and Edgar. It was rated at six h.p., and made 6 m.p.h. on its trial run, July 4.

1895. George B. Selden of Rochester is granted a patent on the "Road Engine" for which he applied in 1879.

The following cars made their first appearance: Electric Wagon, Electrobat, Haynes-Apperson, Hertel, Hill's Locomotor, Hall Gas-oline Trap, Howard Gasoline Wagon, Stanley Steam Car, J. B. West's Gasoline Vehicle.

1896. Charles King completes a car with four-cylinder, four-cycle water-cooled engine, the first automobile on the streets of Detroit. Henry Ford makes his first self-propelled vehicle with a two-cylinder, four h.p. engine. It had no reverse.

Alexander Winton produces an experimental two-seated motor carriage. R. E. Olds appears on the streets of Lansing in a one-cylinder, six h.p. machine.

Other cars making their bow in 1896 were Benton Harbor Motor, Motor Drag, Eisenhuth, Emerson and Fisher's Motor Wagon, Higdon Horseless Carriage, Mueller's Motor Carriage, Riker Electric.

(Packard Motor Car Co. Photo)

"ANYBODY GOT A BLOTTER?"   Incident on one of the Glidden tours.

1897. Olds Motor Vehicle organizes the first automobile company in Michigan.

Studebaker begins experimenting on electric carriages.

Newcomers are: Antohny's Electric Runabout, Barrows Motor Vehicle, Columbia Motor Carriage, Cross's Steam Carriage, Electric Delivery Wagon, Elliott's Motor Carriage, Erie and Sturges Gasoline Carriage, Gasoline Motor Carriage (Sintz), A. L. Morgan's Motor Carriage, Reeve's Motor Carriage, Whitney Steam Wagon.

Note how they cling to the carriage and wagon idea.

1898. The first four-cylinder, valve-in-head air-cooled engine from which Franklin patterned his motor is built by John Wilkinson.

New York City starts an electric car service.

Meet the newcomers: Altham, Brown's Touring Cart, Clapp's Motor Carriage, Empire, General Electric's Carriage, Langan's Motor Carriage, Jones Steam Car, Kennedy Electric Carriage, Lewis Motor Carriage, Marsh, Oakman, Rae Electric Car, Stearns Steam Car, Waltham Steam Vehicles, Waverly Electric, Woods Electric.

1899. The Automobile Club of America is organized. International Harvester comes forth with a high-wheeled gasoline Auto Buggy. U. S. Post Office Dept. experiments with automobile delivery. J. W. Packard of Warren, Ohio builds his first car, naming it the Ohio. Joining in the motor family are these: American Electric Autocar, Baker Electric, Chicago, Eastman Electric, Grout Steamer, Hasbrouck, Henley, Holyoke, International Auto Buggy, Jackson, Kensington, Lane Steamer, Leach, Mobile, Overman, St. Louis, U. S. Motor Vehicle, Wisconsin.

1900 -- Turn of the Century! Fifty-four NEW makes put on the market with production reaching the astounding total of 4,192 units in one year—(less than one day's output now). Notable newcomers are: Auburn, Mack, Knox, Peerless, Rambler, Searchmont, Stearns, White Steamer.

Lesser known are: Automobile Fore-car, Baldwin, Boston, Breer's Steam Car, Buffalo, Buffum, Canada, Century, Clark-Carter, Contrad, Crouch, Foster, Friedman, Gasmobile, Gurley, Hewitt-Lindstrom, Holley, Imperial, Jeffry (not Jeffery), Keene, Klock, Lancaster, Loomis, Marlboro, Media, Milwaukee, Murdaugh, National, New York, Robinson, Skene, Spaulding, Spiller, Springfield, Steam Vehicle, Strathmore, Strong & Rogers, Thompson, Triumph, Waltham (also made Orient Buckboard).

CAPT. M. A. SHUEY, pioneer auto dealer of South Bend and two of the Apperson Jackrabbits he sold. One of his claims is that he established the "first gerridge between Paris and Chicago." Cap's knowledge of geography was a bit hazy.

Capt. Shuey, dealer extraordinary

One of the most colorful of the pioneer dealers was the late Capt. Manlove A. Shuey, of South Bend, whose title had been acquired as skipper of a squat little side-wheeler on the St. Joe River. When a kid he had run away from home to join Brady's Circus of Baraboo, Wisconsin; became a ground tumbler, "blew the tuby" in the band and later, when the Nebraska Indians had come into some Federal money, he sold them some melodeons from the back of a wagon.

With this rich experience behind him, combined with a hospitable nature, a robust imagination and a tongue that hung in the middle, Cap automatically became a raconteur of first water. His fame spread; men in all walks of life came from far and near to be entertained by his yarns, among them Henry Ford himself.

Cap was tall and lean and for years wore same black broadcloth suit, shiny yet neatly brushed; turn-down collar, black bow tie and stiff white dickey setting off a preposterous diamond of finest cut glass. He never would admit that his tan cloth gaiters were spats. The only items he removed when working on a car were a pair of celluloid cuffs; rarely did he put on coveralls, but he always managed to appear neat. To be sure, he did little mechanical tinkering, his talents being pretty much limited to salesmanship of a rather florid character. Liquor didn't appeal to him and beyond certain hand-embroidered profanity of a stimulating quality and addiction to Fast Mail Fine Cut chewing tobacco, he had no vices.

Before I was well acquainted with the subtleties of his nature we made a trip to the Ford plant together. He carried a capacious black valise which, from his impeccable exterior, I naturally assumed contained a neatly folded suit of pajamas, a stack of fresh linen and other accoutrements of the tidy traveler. It shamed my meager overnight bag. En route he had an occasion to open it on the seat between us, revealing its sole contents to be a burnt-out connecting rod, and a ring gear reposing on a heaping mound of Fast Mail tobacco!

It was in 1899 that Cap established a "repository" in back of Hobbs furniture store to handle Mobile steamers, the Friedman and eventually the Ford. Cap claims he sold the third Ford car Henry ever built (it was the 49th) "and I had to lend him eleven dollars and thirty-five cents to buy paint and bolts to finish it up with."

Cap described his meeting with the then unknown Ford many times on request, with improvements at each telling, how he first heard of him through a tire salesman, his difficulty in locating him in Detroit, finally finding him under a half-built chassis in a dingy blacksmith shop.

There was some truth in his claim "Me and Hank got to be right chummy. Why, lots of times he'd come down here (South Bend) just to visit and talk over old times, and never mention a word about business. Once he brought Edsel with him, when the boy was in knee pants."

In Cap's later years Ford gave him a Model T taxi with which to make a living, and after a serious accident he spent a long period in the Ford Hospital, gratis.

Roll Call of 1876 American-Made Automobiles and Trucks

A. B. C.
Abenaque
Abendroth & Root
Abbott
Abbott-Cleveland
Abbott-Detroit
Abbott-Downing
Acadia
Acason
Ace
A. C. F.
Acme
Acorn
Adams
Adams-Farwell
Adelphia
Adria
Adrian
Advance
A. E. C.
Aero
Aerocar
Aerotype
Ahrens-Fox
Ajax, 1901
Ajax, 1925
Akron
Alamobile
Aland
Albany
Alco
Aldo
Alden-Sampson
All American
Allen
Allen & Clark
Allen-Kingston
Allith
All Steel
Alma
Alpena
Alsace
Alter
Altha
Altham
Alxo
Amalgamated
Ambassador
Amco
America
American
American-Bantam
American Beauty
American Benham
American Berliet
American Chocolate
American Coulthard

American Electric
American Fiat
American-LaFrance
American-Mors
American-Simplex
American Underslung
American Voiturette
Ames
Amesbury
Amplex
Ams-Sterling
Anchor
Anderson, 1908
Anderson, 1916
Anger
Angus
Anhut
Anthony's
 Electric Runabout
Apex
Apperson
Apple
Appleton
Appolo
Arbenz
Arcadia
Ardsley
Argo
Argo-Case
Argonne Four
Ariel
Aristos
Armleder
Arrow
Artzberger
Astor
Astra
Atlantic
Atlas
Atlas-Knight
Atterbury Truck
Auburn
Auglaize
Aultman
Aurora
Austin
Auto-Acetylene
Auto-Bug
Autobuggy
Autocar Truck
Autocycle
Autodynamic
Auto-Go
Automatic
Automotor
Autotwo
Auto Vehicle

Available Truck
Avery

B

Babcock
Bachelles Electric
Backhus
Bacon
Badger
Bailey
Baker
Baker Electric
Balboa
Baldner
Baldwin
Ball
Banker
Banker Electric
Bantam
Barbarino
Barley
Barlow
Barnes
Barnhart
Barrow Electric
Bartholomew
Barver
Bateman
Bates
Bauer
Bauroth
Bay State, 1906
Bay State, 1922
Beacon Flyer
Beardsley
Beaver
Bee
Beggs
B. E. L.
Belden
Belfontains
Bell
Belmont
Bemmel & Burnham
Bendix
Benham
Ben-Hur
Benner
Benson
Benton Harbor
Berg
Bergdoll
Berkshire
Bertolet
Berwick Electric
Bessemer Truck
Best
Bethlehem

Betz
Beverly
Bewis
Bewman
Biddle
Biddle-Murray
Biederman Truck
Bimel
Binney-Burnham
Birch
Bird
Birmingham
Black
Black Crow
Black Diamond
Blackhawk, 1903
Blackhawk, 1929
Blair
Blaisdell
Blakeslee
Bliss
B. L. M.
Blomstrom
Blood
Blumberg
Boggs
Boisselot
Bollee
Bolte
Borbein
Borland
Boss
Boston
Boston & Amesbury
Bour-Davis
Bournonville
Bowman
Boynton
Bradfield
Bradley
Bramwell
Bramwell-Robinson
Brasie
Brazier
Brecht
Breeze & Lawrence
Brennan
Brew-Hatcher
Brewster
Brewster-Knight
Bridgeport
Briggs & Detroiter
Briggs & Stratton
Brighton
Brightwood
Brintel
Briscoe

Bristol
Broc Electric
Brock
Brockville-Atlas
Brockway Truck
Brodesser
Brook
Brooks
Brown's Touring Cart
 1898
Brown, 1914
Brown, 1916
Brown-Burtt
Brownell
Browniekar
Brunn
Brunswick
Brush
Bruss
Buck
Buckeye
Buckles
Buckmobile
Buffalo
Buffington
Buffum
Buggaut
Buggycar
Bugmobile
Buick
Burdick
Burg
Burns
Burroughs
Busser
Buzmobile
Byrider

C

Cadillac
California
Californian
Calvert
Cameron, 1903
Cameron, 1914
Campbell
Canda
Cannon
Cantono
Capitol
Carbon
Car DeLuxe
Cardway
Carhart
Carhartt
Carlson
Car-Nation

Roll Call of 1876 Automobiles and Trucks

Carrison
Carrol
Carroll
Carter
Cartercar
Cartermobile
Carthage
Casco
Case
Cato
Cavac
Cavalier
Caward-Dart
Ceco
Celt
Centaur
Central
Century
Century Electric
C. F.
C. G. V.
Chadwick, 1905
Chadwick, 1911
Chalfant
Chalmers
Chalmers-Detroit
Champion, 1909
Champion, 1921
Chandler
Chapman
Charter Oak
Chase
Checker Cab
Chelsea
Chevrolet
Chicago
Chicago Commercial
Chicago Motor Buggy
Chief
Christie
Christman
Christopher
Chrysler
Church
Churchfield
Cincinnati
Cinco
Cino
Clark
Clark-Carter
Clark Electric
Clark-Hatfield
Clarkmobile
Clarkspeed
Classic
Clear & Dunham
Cleburne
Clendon
Clermont, 1903
Clermont, 1922
Cleveland, 1902
Cleveland, 1919
Climber
Clinton
Cloughley
Club Car
Clyde
Clydesdale Truck
Clymer

Coates
Coates-Goshen
Coey
Cogswell
Colburn
Colby
Cole
Coleman Truck
Collinet
Collins
Collins Electric
Colly
Colonial
Colt
Columbia, 1900
Columbia, 1916
Columbia Electric
Columbia-Knight
Columbus
Comet
Commander
Commerce
Commercial
Commodore
Commonwealth
Compound
Concord
Conda
Condor Truck
Connersville
Conover
Conrad
Consolidated
Continental, 1907
Continental, 1933
Cook
Coppock
Corbin
Corbitt Truck
Cord
Corinthian
Corl
Cornelian
Cornish-Friedberg
Correja
Corweg
Corwin
Cosmopolitan
Cotta
Country Club
Couple-Gear
Courier, 1904
Courier, 1909
Courier, 1922
Covert
C. P.
Craig-Hunt
Craig-Toledo
Crane
Crane & Breed
Crane-Simplex
Crawford
Crescent
Crest
Crestmobile
Cricket
Criterion
Crock
Coressus, Jr.

Crompton
Crosley
Cross' Steam
  Carriage
Crouch
Crow
Crowdus
Crow-Elkhart
Crown
Crown-Magnetic
Crowther
Croxton
Croxton-Keeton
Crusader
Crusier
Cucmobile
Cull
Culver
Cunningham, 1901
Cunningham, 1911
Curtis
Custer
Cutting
C. V. I.
Cyclecar
Cyclemobile
Cycleplane

D

D. A. C.
Dagmar
Dalton
Daniels
Dan Patch.
Darby
Darling
Darrow
Dart Truck
Dartmobile
Davenport
Davids
Da Vinci
Davis
Dawson
Day
Day-Elder Truck
Dayton
Day Utility
Deal
Decauville
Decker
Decross
Deemotor
Deemster
Deere
Deere-Clark
Deering
Defiance
DeKalb
Delage
DeLaVergne
Delling
Delmore
Deltal
DeLuxe
DeMartini
DeMot
DeMotte
Denby
Derain

Desberon
DeShaw
DeSoto, 1913
DeSoto, 1928
DeTamble
Detroit, 1900
Detroit, 1922
Detroit-Chatham
Detroit-Dearborn
Detroit Electric
Detroit Speedster
DeVaux
Dewabout
Dey
Dial
Diamond
Diamond-Arrow
Diamond T Truck
Dianna
Diexel
Differential
Dile
Direct Drive
Disbrow
Dispatch
Divco Truck
Dixie
Dixie Flyer
Dixie Tourist
Dixon
Doane Truck
Doble-Detroit
Doble Steam Car

Dodge
Dodge-Graham
Dodgeson 8
Dodo
Dolson
Dorris
Dort
Douglas
Dover
Dowagiac
Downing
Dragon
Drake
Drednot
Drexel

Driggs
Drummond
Duck
Dudley
Duebon

Duer
Duesenberg
Dumont
Dunn

Duplex Truck
DuPont
Duquesne
Durant, 1921
Durant, 1927
Durocar
Duryea
Dusseau
Dyke
Dymaxion

E

Eagle, 1905
Eagle, 1924
Eagle-Macomber
Eagle Rotary
Earl, 1907
Earl, 1921
Eastern Dairies
Eastman Electric
Easton
Eaton
Eck
Eclipse
Economy, 1906
Economy, 1917
Economycar
Eddy
Edwards-Knight
E. H. V.
Eichstaedt
Eisenhuth
Elbert
Elcar
Elco
Eldredge
Electra
Electric Vehicle
Electric Wagon
Electrobat
Electrocar
Electronomic
Elgin
Elinore
Elite
Elite Steamer
Elk
Elkhart
Elliot's Carriage
Ellis
Ellsworth
Elmore
Elwell-Parker
Elysee
Emancipator
Emerson & Fisher
E. M. F.
Empire, 1898
Empire, 1914
Empire State
Empress
Endurance
Enger
Englehardt
Engler
Entiro
Entyre
Entz
Erie
Erie & Sturgis
  Gasoline Carriage
Erskine
Esco Truck
Essex
Essex Steam Car
Euclid
Eureka
Evans
Evansville
Everitt

Roll Call of 1876 Automobiles and Trucks

Everybody's
Ewing

F

Facto
Fageol Bus
Fairbanks-Morse
Fairmount
F. A. L.
Falcar
Falcon
Falcon-Knight
Famous
Fanning Electric
Fargo Truck
Farmack
Farmobile
Farner
Federal
Federal Truck

Fee
Fenton
Fergus
Ferris
Field
Fifth Avenue Coach
Findley
Firestone-Columbus
Fischer
Fish
Flagler
Flanders
Flanders Electric
Flexbi
Flint, 1902
Flint, 1923
Flyer
Foos
Ford
Forest
Forest City
Forster Six
Fort Pitt
Foster
Fostoria
Four Traction
Fox
Frankfort
Franklin
Frayer

Frayer-Miller
Frazer
Fredonia
Fredrickson
Freeman
Fremont
French
Friedman
Friend
Fritchie Electric

Frontenac
Front Drive
Frontmobile
F. R. P.
F. S.
Fuller
Fulton
F. W. D. Truck
Fwick

G

Gabriel
Gadabout
Gaeth
Gale
Galt
Gardner
Garford Truck
Gary Truck
Gas-Au-Lec
Gas Engine
Gasmobile
Gasoline Motor
    Carriage
Gaylord
Gearless, 1907
Gearless, 1921
Gem
General
General Cab
General Electric
General Vehicle
Genesee
Geneva, 1901
Geneva, 1917
German-American
Geronimo
Gersix
Ghent
Gibbs
Gibson
Gifford-Pettitt
Gillette
G. J. G.
Gleason
Glide
Globe
G. M. C. Truck
Goethe
Golden Eagle
Golden State
Goodspeed
Gotfredson Truck
Grabowsky
Graham
Graham-Fox
Graham-Paige
Gramm Truck
Gramm-Bernstein
Gramm-Logan
Grand
Granite Falls
Grant
Grant-Ferris
Grass-Premier
Graves-Condon
Gray
Gray-Dort
Great
Great Arrow
Great Eagle
Great Smith
Great Southern
Great Western
Gregory
Greeley
Grensfelder
Greuter
Greyhound

Gride
Grinnell
Griswold
Grout
Guilder Truck
Gurley
Guy-Vaughan
Gyroscope

H

Hackett
Hahn Truck
H. A. L.
Hale
Hal-Fur
Hall Gasoline Trap
Halladay
Halsey
Halton
Hambrick
Hamilton
Hamlin-Holmes
Hammer
Hammer-Sommer
Handley-Knight
Hanger
Hannah Truck
Hanover
Hansen
Hanson
Harding
Hardy
Harper
Harrie
Harrigan
Harris
Harrisburg
Harrison
Harroun
Hart-Kraft
Hartley
Hartman
Harvard
Harvey
Hasbrouck
Haseltine
Hassler
Hatfield
Hathaway
Havers
Hawkeye
Hawley
Hay-Berg
Haydock
Hayes-Anderson
Haynes
Haynes-Apperson
Hayward
Hazard
H. C. S.
Healy Electric
Hebb
Heifner
Heilman
Heine-Velox
Hendel
Henderson
Hendrickson Truck
Henley
Henney Hearse

Henrietta
Henry
Hercules Electric
Herff-Brooks
Herreshoff
Herschmann
Hertel
Hertz
Hess
Hewitt
Hewitt-Lindstrom
Heymann
Hicks
Higdon & Higdon
Highlander
Hill
Hillsdale
Hill's Locomotor
Hinde & Dauch
Hobbie
Hockenhull
Hoffman
Holden
Holland
Holley
Hollier
Holly
Holmes
Holsman
Hol-Tan
Holton
Holtzer-Cabot
Holyoke
Homer
Homer-Laughlin
Hoosier Scout
Hopkins
Hoskins
Houghton
Houghton Steamer
Houpt
Houpt-Rockwell
House
Howard Gasoline
    Wagon
Howey
Hudson
Hudson Steam Car
Huffman
Hug Truck
Hunter
Huntington
Hupmobile
Hupp-Yeats
Hurlburt
Hydro-Carbon
Hydromotor
Hylander

I

Ideal
Ideal Electric
I. H. C.
Illinois
Imp
Imperial, 1900
Imperial, 1907
Independence
Independent
Indianapolis

Indiana Truck
Ingrame-Hatch
Innes
International Truck
Interstate
Intrepid
Iowa
Iriquois
Iverson

J

Jackson
Jacks Runabout
Jacquet Flyer
James
Janney
Jarrett Truck
Jarvis-Huntington
Jaxon
Jay
Jay-Eye-See
Jeannin
Jeffrey
Jem
Jenkins
Jewell
Jewett, 1906
Jewett, 1922
Johnson
Jones Steam Car
Jones-Corbin
Jonz
Jordan
J. P. L.
Jr.
Julian
Juvenile

K

Kaiser
Kalamazoo
Kane-Pennington
Kankakee
Kansas City
Karbach
Kato
Kauffman
K. D.
Kearns
Keasler
Keene
Keeton
Keller-Kar
Kelley-Springfield
Kellogg
Kelly
Kelsey
Kenmore
Kennedy
    Electric Carriage
Kensington
Kent
Kenworth Truck
Kermath
Kermet
Kerns
Kerosene Surrey
Kessler
Keystone, 1900
Keystone, 1909
Kiblinger
Kidder

Roll Call of 1876 Automobiles and Trucks

Kimball
King
King-Remick
Kingston
King Zeitler
Kinnear
Kinney
Kirk
Kissell
Kleiber Truck
Kline
Kline-Kar
Kling
Klink
Klock
Knickerbocker
Knight & Kilbourne
Knight Special
Know
Knox
Knox-Landsen
Kobusch
Koehler
Komet
Konigslow
Koppin
Kraft
Krall
Krastin
Krebs Truck
Kreuger
K-r-i-t
Kron
Kunz
Kurtz

L

Laconia
Lad's Car
Lafayette
LaFayette
LaFrance-Republic
LaMarne
Lambert
Lamphen
Lancamobile
Lancaster
Lane Steamer
Langan's Motor
    Carriage
Lange Truck
Lanpher
Lansden
La Petite
Larchmont
Larson
LaSalle
Lasky
Laughlin
Laurel
Lauth-Juergens
Law
Lawter
L. C. E.
L & E
Leach
Leach-Biltwell
Leader
Lear
Lebanon
Lehigh

Lehr
Le Moon Truck
Lende
Lennon
Lenox
Lescina
Lewis Motor
    Carriage, 1898
Lewis, 1901
Lewis, 1913
Lexington
Liberty
Liberty-Brush
Lima
Limited
Lincoln, 1911
Lincoln, 1921
Lincoln-Zephyr, 1935
Lindsley
Lion
Little
Littlemac
Locomobile
Logan
Lomax
London
Lone Star
Long
Long Distance
Longest
Loomis
Lorraine, 1907
Lorraine, 1920
Los Angeles
Louisiana
Lowell
Lowell-American
Lozier
L. P. C.
Luedinghaus
Lutz
Luverne
Luxor Cab
Lyman
Lyman & Burnham
Lyon
Lyons-Atlas
Lyons-Knight

M

Maccar
MacDonald
Mack
Mackle-Thompson
MacNaughton
Macomber
Macon
Macy-Roger
Madison
Magic
Magnolia
Mahoning
Maibohm
Mais
Majestic
Malbomb
Malcolm
Malcolm-Jones
Malden
Manexall
Manhattan

Manistee
Maplebay
Marathon
Marble-Swift
Marelock
Marion
Marion-Handley
Mark-Electric
Marlboro
Marmon
Marmon-Herrington
Marquette, 1912
Marquette, 1929
Marr
Marsh, 1905
Marsh, 1920
Marshall
Martin
Martin-Wasp
Marvel
Maryland
Mascotte
Mason
Massachusetts
Massillon
Master
Mather
Matheson
Mathewson
Mathis
Maumee
Maxim
Maxim-Goodridge
Maxwell
Maxwell-Briscoe
Mayer
Mayfair
Maytag
McCarron
McCrae
McCue
McCullough
McCurdy
McDonald
McFarland
McGill
McIntire
McKay
McLaughlin
Mead
Mearo
Mecca
Med-Bow
Medcraft
Media
Meech-Stoddard
Meiselbach
Melbourne
Mel Special
Menard
Menges
Menominee Truck
Mercedes
Mercer, 1909
Mercer, 1931
Merchant
Mercury
Merit
Merkel

Merz
Messerer
Metcar
Meteor, 1902
Meteor, 1914
Metropol
Metropolitan
Metz
Metzger
Michigan
Middleby
Midgley
Midland
Midwest
Mier
Mighty Michigan
Milac
Milburn Electric
Miller
Miller Special
Mills
Milwaukee
Minneapolis
Mino
Mission
Mitchell
Mitchell-Lewis
Mobile
Mock
Model
Modern
Modilette
Modoc
Mogul
Mohawk
Mohler
Moline, 1905
Moline, 1911
Moline-Knight
Moller Cab
Monarch
Moncrief
Mondex-Magic
Monitor
Monroe
Moody
Mooers
Moon
Moore
Mora
More
Moreland Truck
Morelock
Morgan's Motor
    Carriage
Morriss
Morris-London
Morrissey
Morse
Morse Steam Car
Motorcar
Motorette
Motor Truck
Moyea
Moyer
M. P. M.
Mt. Pleasant
Mueller's
    Motor Carriage

Mueller-Benz
Mulford
Multiplex
Muncie
Munson
Murdaugh
Murray
Murray-Mac Six
Mutual

N

Nance
Napier
Napoleon
Nash
National
National Electric
National Sextet
Nebraska
Neilson
Nelson
Netco Truck
Neustadt-Perry
Nevin
Newark
New England Truck
New Era
New Home
New York
Niagara
Nichols-Shepard
Noble Truck
Noma
Norma
Northern
Northway
Northwestern
Norton
Norwalk
Novara
Nyberg

O

Oakland
Oakman
Obertine
O. B. Truck
O'Connell
Offenhauser
Ogden Truck
Ogren
Ohio
Ohio Electric
Ohio Falls
Okey
O. K. Truck
Oldfield
Old Reliable
Oldsmobile
Oliver
Olympian
Olympic
Omaha
Omort
Oneida Truck
Onlicar
Only
Oregon
Orient
Orion
Ormond

Roll Call of 1876 Automobiles and Trucks

Orson
Oshkosh Truck
Otto
Ottokar
Otto-Mobile
Overholt
Overland
Overman
O-We-Go
Owen
Owen Magnetic
Owen-Shoeneck
Owen-Thomas
Oxford

P

Pacific
Packard
Packers
Page
Page-Toledo
Paige
Paige-Detroit
Pak-Age-Car
Palmer
Palmer-Moore
Palmer-Singer
Pan
Pan-American, 1903
Pan-American, 1917
Panther
Paragon
Paramount Cab
Parenti
Parker
Parkin
Parry
Parsons
Partin
Partin-Palmer
Pastoria
Pathfinder
Patriot
Paterson
Paterson-Greenfield
Pawtucket
Payne-Modern
Peabody
Peerless
Pellitier
Peninsular
Penn
Pennington
Pennsy
Pennsylvania
People's
Perfection
Perfex
Perry
Peru
P. E. T.
Peter Pan
Peters
Petrel
Phelps
Phianna
Phipps
Phoenix
Pickard
Piedmont

Pierce
Pierce-Arrow
Pierce-Racine
Piggins
Pilgrim
Pilliod
Pilot
Pioneer
Piscorski
Pitcher
Pittsburgh
Pittsburgh Electric
Planche
Plymouth, 1908
Plymouth, 1928
Pneumobile
Polo
Pomroy
Ponder
Pontiac, 1908
Pontiac, 1925
Pope-Hartford
Pope Motor
Pope-Robinson
Pope-Toledo
Pope-Tribune
Pope-Waverly
Poppy Car
Porter, 1900
Porter, 1915
Port Huron
Portland
Postal
Powercar
Prado
Pratt
Preferred
Premier
Premocar
Prescott
Preston
Pridemore
Primo
Prince
Princess
Princeton
Prospect
Pullman
Pungs-Finch
Puritan
Pyramid

Q

Queen
Quick
Quinlan

R

Rae Electric Car
Railsbach
Rainier
Ralco
Raleigh
Rambler
Randall
Randall Steamer
Randolph
Ranger
Rapid Truck
Rassler
Rauch & Lang Electric

Rayfield
R. C. H.
Read
Reading
Real
Reber
Red Bug
Red Jacket
Red Wing
Reed
Rees
Reeves Motor
  Carriage
Regal
Regas
Rehberger Truck
Reid
Reiland & Bree
Reinertsen
Relay Truck
Reliable
Reliable-Dayton
Reliance
Remal-Vincent
Remmington
Reno
Reo
Republic Truck
Revere
Rex
Reya
Rhodes
Richards
Richlieu
Richmond
Rickenbacker
Ricketts
Riddle
Rider-Lewis
Riess-Royal
Riker Electric
Riley & Cowley
Riper
Ritz
Riveria
R. M. C.
R. O.
Roach
Roader
Roadster
Roamer
Robe
Roberts
Robie
Robinson
Robson
Roche
Rochester
Rockaway
Rocket
Rock Falls
Rockliff
Rockne
Rockwell
Rodgers
Roebling
Roger
Rogers
Rogers & Hanford

Rollin
Rolls-Royce
Roman
Romer
Roosevelt
Roper
Ross, 1905
Ross, 1907
Rotarian
Rotary
Rovena
Rowe
Royal
Royal Tourist
Rubay
Rugby Truck
Ruggles Truck
Ruggmobile
Ruler
Rumley
Runabout
Rush
Rushmobile
Russell
Rutenberg
Ruxton
R & V Knight
Ryder

S

Saf-T-Cab
Saginaw
Salisbury
Salter
Salvador
Sampson
Sandlow
Sandow Truck
Sanford Truck
Sandusky
Santos Dumont
Saurer Truck
Savage
Sawyer
Saxon
Sayers
Sayers & Scoville
Schacht
Schaum
Schlosser
Schnader
Schwartz
Scott
Scott-Newcomb
Scripps
Scripps-Booth
Seabrook
Seagrave
Searchmont
Sears Motor Buggy
Sebring
Sekine
Selden
Selden Truck
Sellers
Senator
Seneca
Serpentina
Serrifile
Service Truck
Severin
S. G. V.

Sha
Shad-Wyck
Shain
Sharon
Sharp-Arrow
Shaum
Shaw
Shawmut
Shaw-Wick
Shelby
Sheridan
Shoemaker
Sibley
Sibley-Curtis
Sigma
Signal
Signet
Silent
Silent Knight
Silver Knight
Simms
Simons
Simplex
Simplex-Crane
Simplicity
Simplo
Sinclair-Scott
Singer
Single Center
Sintz
S. J. R.
Skelton
Skene
S & M
Smith
Smith & Mabley
Smith Motor Wheel
S. N.
Snyder
Sommer
Soules
South Bend
Southern Six
Sovereign
Spacke
Spartan
Spaulding, 1900
Spaulding, 1916
Special
Speedway
Speedwell
Spencer
Sperling
Sperry
Sphinx
Spiller
Spoerer
Springer
Springfield
Sprite
Squier
S & S Hearse
Stafford
Stammobile
Standard
Standard Eight
Standard Electric
Standard Steamer
Stanhope

Roll Call of 1876 Automobiles and Trucks

Stanley
Stanley Steamer
Stanley-Whitney
Stanton
Stanwood
Star, 1908
Star, 1922
Star-Flee Truck
Starin
States
Static Super-Cooled
Staver
Steamobile
Steam Vehicle
Stearns
Stearns-Knight
Stearns Steam Car
Steco
Steel Swallow
Stegeman
Steinhart-Jensen
Stein-Koenig
Steinmetz
Stephens
Sterling Truck
Sterling Knight
Sternberg
Stetson
Stevens-Duryea
Stewart-Coates
Stewart Truck
Stilson
St. Joe
St. Louis, 1899
St. Louis, 1922
Stoddard-Dayton
Stoddard-Knight
Storck
Storms
Stoughton
Stout Scarab
Strathmore
Stratton
Streater
Stringer
Strobel & Martin
Strong & Rogers
Strouse
Struss
Studebaker

Studebaker-E.M.F.
Studebaker-Garford
Sturgis
Sturtevant
Stutz
Stuyvesant
Suburban
Success
Sultan
Summit
Sun
Sunset
Superior
Supreme
Synnestvedt
Syracuse

T

Tally-Ho
Tarkington
Taunton
Templar
Templeton-Dubrie
Terraplane
Tex
Texan
Texas
Texmobile
Thomas Flyer
Thomas-Detroit
Thompson
Thornycroft
Thorobred
Thresher
Tiffany
Tiffin
Tiger
Tillie
Tincher
Titan Truck
Tjaarda
Toledo
Tonawanda
Torbensen
Touraine
Tourist
Tower
Trabold
Traffic
Transport Truck

Trask-Detroit
Traveler
Trebert
Triangle
Tri-Car
Tri-Moto
Trinity
Triunfo
Triumph
Trumbull
Tudhope
Tulsa
Twin City
Twin Coach
Twombly
Twyford

U

Ultimate
Union
United
Universal
University
Unwin
Upton
U. S. Motor Vehicle

V

Valley Dispatch
Van
Van Dyke
Van L.
Vandergrift
Vaughan
V. E. C.
Velie
Vernon
Vestal
Victor
Victoria
Victory
Viking, 1908
Viking, 1929
Vim Cyclecar
Vim Truck
Virginian
Vixen
Vocur
Vogue
Vulcan

W

Wachusett Truck
Waco
Wagenhals
Wahl
Walden
Waldron
Walker Truck
Walls
Walter Truck
Waltham, 1900
Waltham, 1922
Waltham-Orient
Walther
Walworth
Wanamaker
Ward Electric
Ward LaFrance
Ward-Leonard
Warren
Warren-Detroit
Warwick
Washington
Wasp
Waterloo
Waterous
Watt
Waukeshaw
Waverly Electric
Wayne
Weidley
Welch
Welch-Detroit
Welch-Marquette
Welch-Pontiac
Werner Truck
West's Gasoline Vehicle
Westcott
Western
Westfield
Westinghouse
Weston
W. F. S.
Whaley-Henriette
Wharton
Whippet
White Hall
White Hickory
White Star

White Steam Car
White Truck
Whiting
Whitney Steam Wagon
Wichita Truck
Wick
Wilco
Wilcox
Wildman
Will Truck
Willard
Williams
Wills St. Claire
Willys
Willys-Knight
Willys-Overland
Wilson
Windsor
Wing
Winther
Winton
Wisconsin
Witt Will
Wizard
Wolfe
Wolverine, 1904
Wolverine, 1927
Wonder
Woodruff
Woods Dual Power
Woods Mobilette
World Truck
Worth
Worthington
Wright

Y

Yale, 1903
Yale, 1917
Yates
Yellow Cab
Yellow Coach
York
York-Pullman

Z

Zent
Zentmobile
Zephyr
Zimmerman
Zip

ACKNOWLEDGEMENTS

Collecting material for a book of this kind requires dogged perseverance. I began picking up items as early as 1905. Automobile clubs and manufacturers, the Edison Institute and the Smithsonian Institution were particularly cooperative. Among those who made this book possible are:

Al Abernethy
Fred W. Adams
John D. Adams
Hugh Allen
Greville Bathe
C. D. Barker
F. L. Black
Al Bloemaker
Rudolph Campbell
Frank Campsall

Henry Cave
John A. Conde
Howard H. Clark
Floyd Clymer
F. R. Davis
H. Deupree
J. C. Ellsworth
F. G. Farrell
Tod Ford
Charles Frazier

Sam Garber
Tren Garstone
Edward F. Gibbons
E. G. Hagelthorn
C. T. Jeffery
S. J. Keith
J. A. Kerper
R. S. Kretschmer
Dai H. Lewis, Jr.
E. G. Liebold

Patrice Manahan
Lafayette Markle
F. D. McHugh
W. S. McKinstry
Myron Malony
Ken Merrill
E. C. Morton
C. M. Mylecraine
R. E. Olds
Smith Hempstone Oliver

H. F. Olmstead
Dave Packwood
H. B. Peck
W. L. Powlison
T. P. Rhoades
W. A. Scotten
Earl Squires
Linwood B. Shaw
W. C. Steenburg
Billy Taylor

Cecil H. Taylor
Frank A. Taylor
D. W. Tunberg
Mrs. E. R. Tutt
David H. Utley
Bev Webster
Frank Whitehall
Wallace Woodworth
R. M. Van Zandt

Printed in the U. S. A.

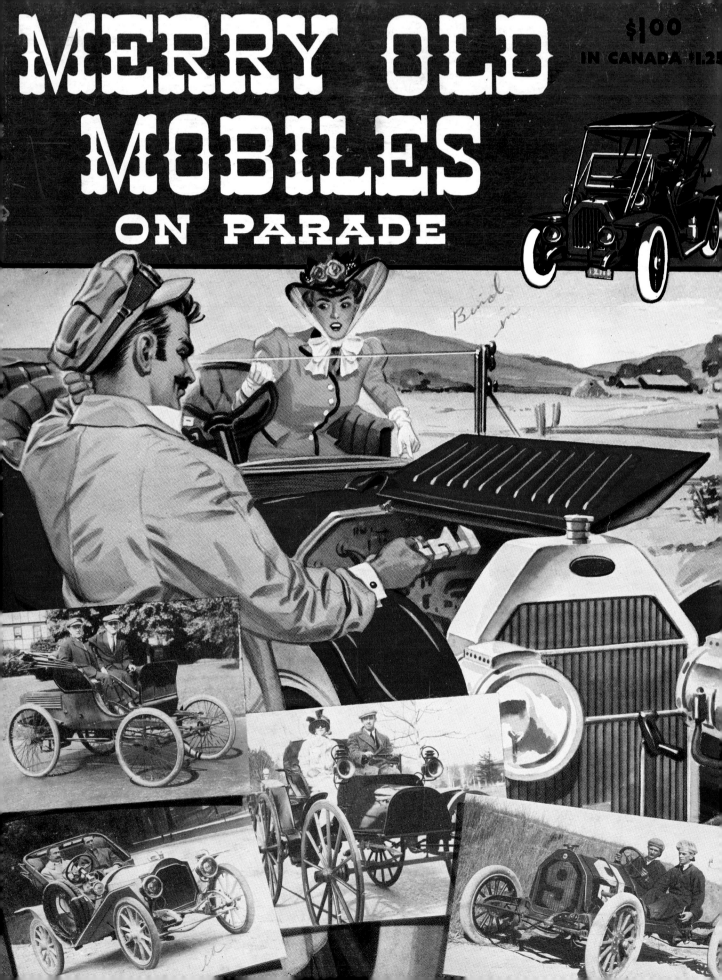